M000211666

ENOUGH IS
ENOUGH!

ENOUGH IS ENOUGH!

I Am The God Who Sees!

A. J. Denzmore

Trilogy Christian Publishers A Wholly Owned Subsidiary of Trinity Broadcasting Network 2442 Michelle Drive Tustin, CA 92780

Copyright © 2020 A.J. Denzmore

No part of this book may be reproduced, stored in a retrieval system or transmitted by any means without written permission from the author. All rights reserved. Printed in USA

Rights Department, 2442 Michelle Drive, Tustin, CA 92780.

Trilogy Christian Publishing/ TBN and colophon are trademarks of Trinity Broadcasting Network.

For information about special discounts for bulk purchases, please contact Trilogy Christian Publishing.

Trilogy Disclaimer: The views and content expressed in this book are those of the author and may not necessarily reflect the views and doctrine of Trilogy Christian Publishing or the Trinity Broadcasting Network.

Manufactured in the United States of America

10 9 8 7 6 5 4 3 2 1

Library of Congress Cataloging-in-Publication Data is available.

B-ISBN#: 978-1-64773-326-1

E-ISBN#: 978-1-64773-327-8

DEDICATIONS

My Heavenly Father

The day that I removed my expectations, my plans, and my visions for my life—then, and only then, did He speak, "Write the book!" Thank you, Father, for showing me Your way! To You, God, be the glory! For You are the God who sees!

To Momma

I dedicate this book to my mother, the most humble, loving woman I have ever known. I love you and miss you so much! To you, for the things you endured because you didn't have a voice. I want to tell you, Momma, that it's okay—all things worked together for the good. Thank you for praying and for loving us! You cried out, and God heard your cry!

To Women

Forgive yourselves because He has forgiven you! Don't worry about what others think about you; Romans 8:1 (KJV) says, "There is therefore now no condemnation to them which are in Christ Jesus, which walketh not after the flesh, but after the Spirit." No more guilt, condemnation, or shame. Get off the cross! You are loved and created in His image! You are beautifully and wonderfully made! Love God, love yourself, and love others!

INTRODUCTION

This is the true story of a woman who is called Anna, whose journey from the womb to the tomb was filled with trauma and pain. Anna's name means "full of grace," and it was by the grace given to her by God that she survived every attack, every obstacle, and even the mistakes that she made. Refusing to give up or give in, she endured, persevered, and proceeded to become more than a conqueror through Christ Jesus. She came forth out of her mother's womb lifeless, but God had already known that day would not be the end of her story. See, no devil in hell can stop the plan or will of God on your life. Destiny was calling her, and as an embryo in her mother's womb she was predetermined to come forth.

Destined to live, and not die, to declare the glory of God! God had a plan for Anna's life, and no matter what Satan did, it would not prevent it from coming to pass. Anna learned obedience by the things she suffered. She had to die to the things of this world, because Anna was standing in her own way. It is God's way, not our way, that we must choose. He is the King of kings, not Burger King! He knew everything she would do before she did it, and He also knew why she was doing it. He knew that through blood, sweat, and tears, she would not allow anyone to stop her from doing the will of God once she was His. Nothing shall separate us from the love of God!

It is written in Romans 8:38-39 (NIV), "For I am convinced that neither death nor life, neither angels nor demons, neither the present nor the future, nor any powers, neither height nor depth, nor anything else in all creation, will be able to separate us from the love of God that is in Christ Jesus our LORD." We have been justified, and now we need to make sure that others are justified. The different situations in Anna's life are bits and pieces of someone else's life, which is why this book was written: to help someone. Somewhere, someone is going through what Anna went through. The solution is life on God's terms. Finally, after enough hell, she surrendered to the will of God and was transformed into His image!

It was no longer Anna that lived, but Christ who lived within her. God is the God who sees the afflictions of His people. He sees the pain of our past, present, and future. God is not just a God who sees. When He sees, He does something about what He sees! In Exodus 3:7 (NKJV), the fact that God sees is confirmed: "And the LORD said: 'I have surely seen the oppression of My people who are in Egypt (bondage), and have heard their cry because of their taskmasters, for I know their sorrows.'" God brought His people out of Egypt's bondage.

God is setting His people free; change has come. The Lord says, "Enough is enough; this is not the plan that I, the Lord thy God, had for the family! I am the God of generations: Abraham, Isaac, and Jacob! This is not the generation that I had in My mind's eye, My vision for My creation. I am restoring the family to its original function using My firm foundation. Enough is enough!" Dying to your will, let it begin in the womb and rise from the tomb! Anna was chosen by God, and no matter what she had done, God chose her—and has chosen you. God's Word will not return to Him void; He said it, and that settles it.

We, as the children of the Most, High God, must know that people are hurting by being abused, battered, beaten, broken, and shattered daily, whether we see it or not. This is not to blame or convict anyone. We have no heaven or hell to put anyone in. It is written in Ephesians 6:12 (KJV), "For we wrestle not against flesh and blood, but against principalities, against powers, against the rulers of the darkness of this world, against spiritual wickedness in high places." It's a spirit and it's just hidden in the dark. It is no longer about "our four and no more"! I pray that this book will take the scales off of our eyes and remove the masks in order to deliver, heal, encourage, strengthen, and restore those who have endured such trauma that only God can heal. Anna got in God's way! Anna went through bad to get to good just to inform someone, anyone, that the best is yet to come. If one life or one family is changed or encouraged, her story has done more than was ever imagined. I'm so thankful to God for delivering me and making me new. We must repent and turn from our wicked ways! ***Enough is enough! I am the God who sees!***

TABLE OF CONTENTS

Chapter 4: Transformed into His Image

Chapter 5: Revealed Knowledge

FORWARD

In some writings, there is art imitating life—and then there is Enough is Enough! Where life is far from art, and the beauty of childhood, adolescence, and adulthood seems unobtainable. It is true that most childhoods are a time of innocence, naiveté, love, joy, and discovery, but where does one run when their childhood is stolen? Where does one look to redeem an unused childhood? What becomes of that person who walks through the rest of their life searching for stolen innocence? Enough is Enough! answers these questions. Once in a generation we are so moved by words on pages, then comes Enough is Enough! From childhood scars to adult healing, it takes a lifetime for some scars to heal. This journey of one woman's life through rejections, mistakes, setbacks, and a series of unfortunate events tells of a faith that triumphantly rescues one from despair. Life is, as one writer wrote, "a tale never told." Enough is Enough! is finally the tale told about life. In this one book, the power of God is displayed to move one from despair to hope, from desperation to freedom, from devastation to victory. Enough is Enough! is a recipe for overcoming life's challenges. This book is for everyone—mothers, fathers, parents, women, men, married, single, divorced, alone—there is a chapter for you. In short, Enough is Enough! is the quintessential piece of literary writing that will change the life of every reader.

—Pastor Byron and Lady Eliaka Thompson

Lighthouse of Hope Church, Belleville, IL

CHAPTER 1

ANNA'S JOURNEY BEGINS

FROM THE WOMB

It was January 2, 1962, in East St. Louis, IL. Mrs. Dottie was being rushed to Saint Mary's Hospital. She knew in her heart that she was going to lose another baby, while wondering why she kept allowing this to happen. She was rushed to the emergency room, yet again praying to God that she wouldn't lose this baby—thinking of all the other babies she had lost due to the abuse and the choices she had made. Where could she have gone that he wouldn't have found her? The guilt and condemnation were eating away at the very fiber of her soul. Mrs. Dottie was crying, "Not again, Lord, not again," while reflecting on all the times that her babies had kicked in her womb.

Mrs. Dottie remembered her baby boy's face when she was holding his lifeless body. He had made it out alive but wasn't strong enough to survive. "What have I done?" she asked, while praying, "Lord, have mercy on me! Help me, Lord—please help me, Lord! Please, Lord, not this baby too!" Mrs.

Dottie—battered, beaten, bleeding, broken, and bruised—was screaming, with tears flowing down her face, praying, "Lord, have mercy on me! Enough is enough!"

This baby came out of the womb lifeless, not breathing, even after the doctors had tried numerous times to revive her. Her little head was swollen, and she was dead. The doctors said, "Mrs. Dottie, I'm sorry, but she didn't make it. We tried everything we could. She just wasn't strong enough to survive. Mrs. Dottie, that fall you took damaged her brain. Your baby's head is enlarged. The fluids on her brain caused too much damage. Even if she had survived, she would have been brain dead or would have had serious brain damage. She's gone; I'm sorry!" Mrs. Dottie cried out, "Father God, help me!"

I want to take a moment to tell you that your situation could be covered in blood, lifeless, and declared dead—but don't give up. It's not over until God says it's over! God breathes on death!

NO MORE CASUALTIES

"Thus saith the Lord God unto these bones; Behold, I will cause breath to enter into you, and ye shall live" (Ezekiel 37:5 KJV).

Where there is war, there are always casualties—but God, not this time! It's not over until God says it's over. God breathed life back into Anna after all the doctors had said. She was gone—but He is God, and He has the final say. While the doctors were talking, they heard a cry, a loud baby cry. Her mother began to praise God. It was her baby, whom they had said was dead. It was impossible! Minutes were gone; too much time had passed. Mrs. Dottie couldn't recall how long it had been. It was impossible. "It's a girl; she lives." No one could deny that! Mrs. Dottie named her "Anna," after her husband's aunt. Anna was immediately taken into surgery to remove some of the fluids from her body and brain.

The doctors informed Mrs. Dottie, "The baby can't possibly make it through the night; accept that fact, Mrs. Dottie." Well, Anna made it through surgery, and they sent her to intensive care. She was in critical condition. For three months she was in intensive care, still receiving negative reports. One negative report after another; you would think that what the doctors had seen with their own eyes would have shown them that Anna was here to stay. Doctors look at the natural (scientific reality), not the spiritual (miraculous fact). That weapon didn't prosper. *Enough is enough! I am the God who sees!*

Before Anna was formed, God knew her. God predestined ("before knew") her. Anna's journey was already paved to be a conqueror, fighting to survive. Anna knew war before she came forth out of her mother's womb. Anna was a part of a big family of eight (four boys, four girls). Her mother was pregnant fifteen times, and painfully, seven of her siblings were miscarried, or were born yet didn't survive.

The truth of the matter is that it was from the abuse of her father. You see, her mother was a victim of domestic violence. Her seven siblings (embryos/infants) who died were between Anna and her older siblings. Her older siblings were Arthur Jr., Carlton, Tina, and Carolyn. Tina, who was nine years older than Anna, was the one who informed her about their beautiful baby brother who was born between Carolyn and Anna. He made it out of the womb but wasn't strong enough to survive.

Carlton sat with Anna, sharing the many tragic stories of how their father had abused their mother. Carlton hated how their father had treated their mother, but there was nothing he could do about it. He and Arthur Jr. ("Skeet") would beg her to call the police, and she would tell them, "Shut your mouth; that is your father!" They were not even allowed to tell her family, and their mother kept it hidden in the dark. You see, what went on in their house stayed in their house. What would things have been like if someone could have, or would have, told anyone what was going on? That Anna's father was an alcoholic, an adulterer, a "ho-monger," a gambler, and a womanizer were just a few of his problems, but he was loved and didn't know it. The abuse is a prime example of how hurting people hurts people. *Enough is enough!*

Their mother was a humble woman who believed in "until death do us part." Did she ever think that her death would them part? Anna's mother loved God, her husband, and her children. Everyone knew that fear was a big part of it. What kind of love was this? God only knows the unseen, unspoken traumas, because we know it didn't begin then. There's a new day on the horizon. There may not have been a lot of options then, but there are now. Seek help—it is there for you! *Enough is enough! I am the God who sees!*

ANNA IS NUMBER EIGHT

What Satan meant for evil, God turned for the good. Anna was dead, and she was the number eight child to die by the hands of her father—but God said, "Not so!" The number eight was the new beginning and seven was the completion; it was finished. In the book of Genesis, eight is where God remembered Noah on the ark. The number eight represents a new order and a change of events. God heard the cry of Anna's mother! Anna lived to declare the glory of God, because God breathed life back into Anna; no more shall die by the hands of her father.

A new beginning was on the horizon! Anna was finally allowed to be weighed, because the fluids on her brain and in her body had finally decreased. Anna's mother said, "When you were born, you were over twelve pounds, but when the fluids were removed, you were at nine pounds." Anna eventually got well enough to go to the pediatric ward. The last report that Anna's mother received from the doctors was that she would never live to see two years old. Anna never had to see those doctors again! *Enough is enough! I am the God who sees!*

THE DOOR BEST KEPT CLOSED:

REJECTION

In the hospital, in the midst of isolation, neglect, and loneliness—which is all from the spirit of rejection—the father's rejection of Anna began. The Oxford Dictionary informs us that *rejection* (the noun form) means the absence of a person's affections. It also means to cast aside (set aside). Rejection entered Anna through her mother's womb. Her father's intentions to not have another child by her mother caused Anna to feel those feelings, though she hadn't laid eyes on him yet. The spirit is unseen, yet present. While in her mother's womb, from the abuse of her father bestowed upon her mother, it was inevitable that under the circumstances that spirit would enter in.

The root of the matter: Joyce Meyer, the phenomenal author of *The Root of Rejection,* informs, "Just a little rejection can cause a wound to the soul that will open a door, and through that open door the devil can bring in a spirit of rejection that will rule a person's life. Some of the causes of rejection are unwanted conception, abandonment, being a victim of circumstances, including extended illness following birth that requires hospitalization, and a list of others." Close that door of rejection, please!

Anna's mother didn't receive the affection needed during the pregnancy, and neither did she. Though her mother came to see her whenever she could, her mother's attention was also needed at home, which left very little time for Anna. The attention that Anna did receive from the nurses was minimal, due to their arms being full attending to other infants. Anna's parents loved her! Her mother just couldn't be in two places at one time.

There have been studies on infants divided into two groups: those who received nourishment without affection, and those who received nourishment with affection; the ones that received affection flourished, but the others didn't grow and mature as fast as the other babies. When Anna was finally able to go home, she was still very sick, but guess who came home too? Her father was at home every day. Her mother believed that it was because of the guilt. He had to look into the face of his baby girl and know why she was sick! His baby girl had died, was brought back to life, and had suffered great pain due to his issues. He had to face what he had done to Anna, to her mother, and to the seven infants that never made it home. *Enough is enough!*

Anna's mother became pregnant again. Reginald was born; they were eleven months apart (January to December). Anna still needed to be connected to someone. She lacked social, emotional, and physical healing. There needed to have been an emotional bond between her and her mother. The scars of isolation, neglect, and rejection were never diminished by being replaced with a mother's touch. Reginald and Anna were so close in age; everyone thought they were twins, but they weren't. Anna would climb into the crib with Reginald to touch him, or if he would cry, she had to get to him. Anna needed to touch and to be touched by love!

Two more siblings came after Reginald. There was Bernita, then came Tyrone. Later, as Anna grew older, she wondered how her mother did it with her heart in pieces. She never asked why, because she began to know more about her father. What he wanted, he got. There were four siblings before Anna and three after her. How would her mother be able to spread herself so thin amongst so many needs? Did her father realize that she needed him? Did he understand that Anna's mother could only do so much? *Enough is enough!*

DADDY, WHERE ARE YOU?

Their father was always missing in action. "Papa was a rollin' stone/Wherever he laid his hat was his home" was not an understatement. Wherever he laid his hat was literally his home. Anna's father, while he was married to their mother Dottie, also had two other families. I guess eight children weren't enough for him. Once Anna was old enough to understand that song by the Temptations, "Papa was a Rollin' Stone," she hated it. There was Ms. Martha, who bore him seven children, and Ms. Nancy, who bore him four children. These women knew that he was married, but that didn't stop them; they were drawn into his lust. Some of the children were close to the ages of Dottie's children. One of Dottie's children was born one day after Ms. Martha's child. Anna's mother stated years later that these women would call the house for her husband, but there was nothing she could do about it. You would almost think that he went from one home to the other, night after night. There is no good in causing someone else pain, known or unknown. *Enough is enough!*

Anna's father had nineteen children, and he needed these children to know about each other—especially as they were getting older, if you know what I mean. Eventually, fate played a major role in the process of revealing secrets. The concept of "what goes on in the dark" doesn't stay in the dark. "What you don't know won't hurt you" is a lie from the pit of hell! This is the enemy's way to keep you lying, to okay deception! Anna's sister Carolyn was in elementary school, and their father decided he was going to visit his daughter Diana. Well, as their father walked into the classroom, Carolyn and Diana (Martha's daughter) both stood up and shouted, "Daddy!" Carolyn wasn't the only child he had in that class—surprise, surprise!

Anna's half-sister Diana stood up and shouted "Daddy," too! That secret was out, along with many others. They both looked at each other while he was trying to explain this awkward situation, and you know that tempers were flaring up. Wow, it was on! Their mother always knew that there were other women. But she didn't know, or want to know, the extent of her husband's infidelity. For those who think that they can get away with sin and that it won't come to light, they are wrong. Don't let this be a lesson taught in your child's classroom!

Anna's father had to inform their mother what had happened at the school, and what he had been doing in their marriage for years. Their mother said, "He didn't want his children to date or marry someone and not know about it until it was too late. The act of adultery was crazy enough; let's not add incest." Now Anna knew why her mother was always so sad and cried so much. Anna's mother's pain was more than they could've ever imagined. The man she loved divided himself between three known households. When their father was home, it was long enough to have sex, get her pregnant, eventually beat most of them out of her, and leave. He didn't want the seven babies he killed, but he did want their children. Not one of them was beaten or lost by his hands. God created His souls to be loved and valued; I wonder if anyone ever told Anna's mother that. If a parent is missing, someone is bound to step into those shoes! "Where are you, Daddy?"

CHAPTER 2

DADDY, YOU'RE MISSING IN ACTION

Anna was six years old, and their family was planning a huge celebration for Arthur Jr. (Skeeter), her older brother, who had just come home from the Army. Arthur Jr. had just had his twenty-first birthday, and that was a big thing for their family. He was the hero in the family. He was Anna's hero! Whenever Arthur Jr. came through the door, he would give Anna the biggest hugs. He was so tall that he looked like a giant to her. No matter what was going on around her, she was never afraid in his presence. In Anna's family, there was a lot of arguing—except when Arthur Jr. was home.

The day of the celebration was finally upon them! Everyone was happy, singing, dancing, and laughing, which had been rare for a while. The celebration was at Forest Park and the St. Louis Zoo. They had the grills fired up. The coolers were filled to the fullest, and the tables were filled with side dishes and watermelon. It was on! They had never seen their mother so happy. It was her oldest son's birthday celebration and his visit home from the service. Anna remembered the day he got home. He was wearing his military uniform. He looked so heroic. He no longer had his processed hair (a process for a black man was a permed wave) and he was as sharp as a tack.

"He's sharp as a tack" is a black colloquialism meaning uniformed, creased, ironed, crisp.

Their mother was so proud. She was smiling from ear to ear. She was boasting about her son to all she knew. Their father must have been at his other home. They had separated since the cheater's lesson at her sister's school. What could go wrong on a day like that day? What could happen that would change the course of their destinies? Sometimes we must be careful whom we allow to come near our loved ones. I guess their mother thought that no one could be worse than their father. Little did she know that there was someone more sinister who had entered in through the gate. Who had left the gate open, their father or their mother? Evil is always present.

It was getting late. Everyone was full, and some of them not just from food. Remember, I told you the coolers were filled; it wasn't just pop. I think these drinks are considered "spirits." Well, these spirits came in like a flood! All of their families loaded up and went home. Their mother's friend decided that he wasn't ready for the evening to come to end. Mr. Ed followed their mother to their home. When Anna met Mr. Ed, she was afraid of him; it was something about his eyes. It's been said, "The eyes are the window to the soul of a man." A child can sense danger better than adults can, because they don't see the outer man. They sense the inner man (the spirit and soul), and so does God. Their mother being a beautiful, black woman living in a big house with kids, and no man around, was Mr. Ed's way in! He didn't care that she was married—just the fact that she was alone was enough for him. Their mother couldn't have known how this evening would end. Evil was lurking and persistent in the destruction of this family!

After arriving home, their mother made them all go to bed. All other companies had left except one: Mr. Ed. He and their mother started arguing. Anna jumped out of bed; looking down the hallway, she saw her mother crying and screaming at Mr. Ed. Then she screamed at Anna go to bed, and she ran and lay down, but all of her other siblings were up. She jumped up again and saw the phone broken, which hung on the wall in the hallway. She believed her mother was calling for help. Arthur Jr. (Skeeter) returned and realized that his mother was in danger.

Their mother had broken the phone when she had hit Mr. Ed to make him let her go. Mr. Ed fled from the house, and Skeeter went after him. Their mother was screaming, "Don't go!" Why did he go, and where was their father? Later, Carlton (Anna's brother) told her that their mother had called their father and informed him what was going on before it got out of hand, but he had said no. Their father had told her that he was in bed and he wasn't getting up. Skeeter had also called their dad. He had said that it was his mother's business, not his. Then their dad had hung up the phone! Everything escalated after that, and Skeeter went after Mr. Ed to talk some sense into him. Mr. Ed ran into the vacant house next door.

Skeeter didn't know that Mr. Ed had taken a knife from their kitchen when he ran out the back door. Skeeter ran into the vacant home and up the steps, and Mr. Ed was standing there. The house was dark. Suddenly, Mr. Ed stabbed Skeeter in the chest. He fell down the steps, screaming. The police were called and didn't get there in time. Anna remembered seeing police, hearing sirens, seeing ambulances, and hearing everyone screaming and crying.

Anna ran out and saw a white bed with Skeeter on it, with a lot of blood on him, rolled by two men and put into the ambulance. Anna called out, but Skeeter didn't answer. His eyes were closed, tears running down the side of his face. Their mother's screams were like nothing Anna had ever heard before. All she could hear was her mother screaming, "My baby, my baby, my baby!" Skeeter had been forced to wear shoes he was never meant to wear!

Where there is no man in the house, someone will try to fill those shoes. Skeeter was always a peacemaker. Though Skeeter was in the Army and trained to kill, his training could never have prepared him for this. Though he was twenty-one, he didn't know the devices of wickedness, the dangers of lust, nor the delusional power of an alcoholic. Skeeter had run after him to talk to him, to calm him down, to let him know it was over, and to let bygones be bygones. It wasn't over for Mr. Ed. Anna cried, "Get Daddy—where is he?"

"Please find Daddy; we need Daddy—where is he? I need my Daddy," cried Anna. He was nowhere; Daddy always showed up late, if at all. Their brother, Arthur Jr. (Skeeter), was no more. Their mother later told them what had happened; their father was notified and eventually showed up. Anna remembered the funeral, where they all dressed in black and white. In black bottoms and white tops, sitting from oldest to youngest on the first row next to their mother and father. Skeeter was gone. She had lost her hero. The one who would pick her up to give her a hug and kiss, who told her she was a princess and how pretty she was. Their lives were never the same. First their father, then their brother, and now their mother—where are you? We need you! *Enough is enough*!

The murder of Skeeter changed everything in their family. No one was the same; they had gone from dysfunctional to devastated. How could they go from abundant laughter to abundant pain, all in one day? The day had been a beautiful day—on a scale it had been a one hundred, but it had dropped to a zero instantly. For several years, they didn't hear laughter in their home. There was so much pain. Anna still can hear her mother saying, "Stop all that laughing before something bad happens." That beautiful woman slowly began to diminish.

She was living with the guilt. If she had not allowed that man to come into her life, she would still have had her son. Skeeter was her child, her firstborn.

I'm sure that during the hardest times, he was wiping the tears from her face as they both endured life's pains together. He was the one who decided, "I will go into the Army so that I can get away from all this pain and get my Momma out of East St. Louis, and I will protect my country." He was the one who went into a war, then came home to a war that was not his to fight, and they had lost him. Anna's mother knew that she had to move, even on broken pieces.

WE MOVED ON BROKEN PIECES

Their father never came back home after the murder of Anna's brother. His namesake was gone; the guilt—that he could have made a difference and didn't—kept him from moving forward. We all make choices that we can never undo. Their father's pain became more than he could bear. Their family remained in that house long enough to see several families move into the vacant house, then immediately move out. When neighbors moved into the vacant house where he got stabbed, they complained that around the same time every night they would hear someone running up steps, a scream, and someone falling down the steps.

Eventually, their mother told the neighbors what had happened to her son, and shortly after, they were packed up and gone too. Their mother told the next family also, but they didn't care; they moved in anyway. Strangely, they moved out within a week, saying the same thing: the running up steps, the scream, and the noise of falling down the steps. Finally, their mother knew that she had to move after realizing that his spirit would remain in that house, crying out for her. May Arthur Jr. rest in peace, now.

They moved, but that didn't end the pain. Though they moved, the school was the same, and everyone remembered what had happened to Anna's family. Their mother withdrew even more. Once, when Anna was eight years old, visiting her father's aunt that was her namesake, her aunt spoke evil about their mother. Anna, Angela (her half-sister), and her niece Thea (Skeeter's daughter) were in the living room playing. Anna went into the kitchen to ask for some water; she overheard her Auntie talking to Ms. Martha on the phone. What Anna overheard shocked her. She was talking about Anna's mother. Auntie was telling Ms. Martha that she had told Arthur not to marry her mother, and that he had never loved Dottie. Anna stood there staring at her Auntie from behind (if looks could kill!); then she turned and saw Anna. Nothing much was said between the two after that day. Anna told Angela what was said, and she replied, "Don't mind, Auntie; she talks about everyone." Anna knew that she wasn't safe there. *Enough is enough! I am the God who sees!*

Anna watched her mother cry out to God for hours. She wanted so badly to make her mother happy. Though she still had health issues and wasn't allowed to take gym classes in school, she loved singing and dancing. As a child, when their family came over to visit their mother, she would always call Anna into the living room to sing and dance. Anna can still hear her mother's voice, "Anna Jean, come in here and do your James Brown." This seven-year-old little girl would sing, "I feel good/I knew that I would/I feel good/I knew that I would now/So good, so good/Because I got you!" Then she would do the James Brown slide while pointing her finger at her mom. Her mother loved it, and so did her friends. Anna was great at it.

They eventually moved to the projects. These projects were in East St. Louis, not Miami. They were in a foreign area, "the 'hood." It was a clean area with so many kids, but it was different. Anna's mother was in and out of hospitals. Anna was now nine years old, and three years had come and gone since the death of their brother. Their family never had to worry about chains on the doors, sticks in the windows, and two-by-four boards under the doorknobs. Someone should have told Anna's family what to prepare for. If someone would've warned them, maybe Anna would have never lost what made her so unique!

WHO STOLE ANNA'S SONG AND DANCE?

Anna was getting used to her life in the projects. It wasn't so bad—there were nice homes all around the projects, and across the street there were horses, roosters, and chickens. Grand Farms was in the middle of the 'hood! Everyone knew their neighbors, and her friends were awesome. They had great families, and their dads were home. They were like the *Leave it to Beaver*, *The Brady Bunch*, *Good Times*, and *The Cosby Show* families, having dinner at the same time. At this time, Anna's father was still MIA. He did call Anna to say that he was going to pick her up—she sat on the curb waiting until it got dark, and he never showed up. She cried, and she never got over it.

Anna had a best friend named Emma. Her family was rich and had more than anyone on that block. Her daddy drove a white Cadillac, and he didn't play. Emma told Anna that her daddy had a gun and showed it to her. Back then, when your parents said, "Don't touch," you didn't touch. We looked and didn't touch! Emma's mother was a stay-at-home mom; when her father got home, his plate was ready for him, she had on a beautiful dress, her face was made up, and she wore red lipstick. Anna thought to herself: *This is the life; they made it—yep, they're rich!* Only one strange thing: at the end of the night, they went into two different bedrooms. Anna never questioned Emma about it; at least her father was there with a gun, protecting his family. The next morning Anna left her friend's home, singing, dancing, and wishing her daddy was around.

Where was Anna's protection? Anna wished her mother would have known to put sticks in the window. Anna and her little sister, Bernita, shared a room at the top of the steps of their apartment. Bernita loved sneaking staying up late, and once she fell asleep, she was knocked out—nothing could wake her except their mother's belt. Anna heard a loud noise from downstairs. It was so dark in their home, and she didn't see anything. She thought it was one of her brothers. She asked Bernita, "Did you hear that?" Her sister didn't respond, so Anna went back to sleep.

Later, Anna was awakened by a big man standing over her. It was so dark that she couldn't see his face yet. He put his hands over her mouth and told her to be still. He said, "SHH-HHHH!" Anna tried to wake up her little sister by moving the bed. She wouldn't wake up. He said to her, "If you make a sound, I'll kill you!" Then she realized that she had seen the man before. His name was Joe. He said, "If you make another sound, I will kill your momma!" That's when she stopped.

She knew that if he could get into their home this time, he could come in again. He said, "Where is Carolyn's room?" He had his hand over Anna's mouth. She couldn't say anything. At times, she couldn't breathe. Anna looked in the direction of her mother's room, which was down the hall. At once, he pulled Anna down to the floor! All she thought was, *Doesn't he see my sister? Wake up, Bernita!* Anna couldn't believe what was happening. Time stood still in hell! *It hurt me! Why?* Silently she cried, *Why? Momma, please help me!* No one helped Anna! ***Enough is enough! I am the God who sees!***

There was suddenly a sound in the house like someone was getting up. He stopped and took off running! She screamed and screamed, but no one heard her. She was in shock, in pain; time stood still. Anna kept screaming until her mother finally heard her. She was drowsy from her medicine. Anna said, "Momma, somebody broke into the house!" Her mother ran through the house, down the steps, and saw that the back door was wide open. Then she called the police.

There was Anna, standing in a corner, shaking. The police were searching the home. They noticed the footprint on the front living room windowpane where he broke the lock and came in. Police were asking her mother, "Was anything taken?" The police asked her mother if she was okay, and did she see anything missing? Her mother said, "I'm okay; nothing is missing!" The police asked Anna, "Did you see anything?" She said, "No!" She remembered what he had told her: "SHH-HHH, if you say anything I will come back and kill your momma!" Anna said no again. The police filled out a report and told her mother, "Since nothing was taken, we're leaving, and get a stick for that window once it's fixed!" Anna was standing in the same spot, thinking, *He took something, he did something!* Silently she screamed, *He hurt me!*

Anna saw him one time after that, because he lived in the same projects. Anna was screaming inside! He would not have broken into Emma's house; her father would've been waiting for him. Well, a couple of weeks later he broke into someone else's home and went to prison. His jail sentence didn't and couldn't replace what he had taken from Anna. He had robbed Anna, which was the beginning of a series of horrific events. Hadn't she been through enough already? Things that were once fun, like singing and dancing, were gone. ***Enough is enough!***

Anna wondered, who could she tell? She would sit in class and not hear anything the teachers were saying. She started changing. She went from making paper doll clothes to thinking that no man would hurt her again. She started making vows. She would never get married. She would be a model and travel all over the world. She swore that no man would ever hurt her! Her body started changing, and so did her desires. Miss America pageants were more important! She thought that only the projects had danger. Anna was wrong.

Anna thought junior high school was it! She had arrived! One day after class, she decided that she would go over to her friend's Diane's house. Anna was supposed to go home after school, but instead of skipping school, she skipped going home. At least just for a few minutes. Anna was twelve years old and thought she was "all that." This day, Diane's oldest brother answered the door. Something didn't feel right; it was very quiet. That was never the case in their house. Danger alert, danger alert, danger alert!

Danger greeted Anna at the door! He said, "Come in; Diane will be right back!" When Anna went into their home, such a fear came over her as he drew closer. Anna said, "I will come back when she's home." He said, "No, you can stay," and pushed her down. She knew that she had messed up. She kept saying no. He wasn't listening. She screamed, but nobody heard her! As he raped her, she remembered that a vacant house was next door. Who will hear you, Anna? Not again! When he finished, he acted as if nothing had happened. Not, "I'm sorry!" All Anna kept thinking was, *Not again*! She picked up the pieces and left. ***Enough is enough***!

Anna thought that if she had just gone home, this would've never happened. *I deserved that—if I had only obeyed*! Let's get something straight right now: No one has a right to violate, hurt, nor assault you! No matter what you've done. How could she tell her mother that she went to her friend's house after school, instead of going home like she was supposed to, and she was raped? Anna didn't want to see her mother hurt more than she already had been. Where could she go?

Was anywhere safe? Whom could she trust? *Daddy, where are you?* Anna decided, *I will find you, Daddy, no matter where you are! I need you!* Anna began to search for her daddy. She remembered the other families he had, so maybe if she went to their houses, she would have her daddy. Anna felt that she didn't have anyone she could tell. I know it hurts, but find someone you can trust and tell! You are not alone!

HOME AWAY FROM HOME

Anna began to hang out at one of her father's homes so that she could see him more. It worked! Anna just needed to see her daddy! Ms. Martha's house was where he had seven children, and it became her second home. A lot of times, Anna felt that she was betraying her mother, but she needed him. She had a lot of fun at Ms. Martha's house; her daddy was hardly ever there, and even when he was, he wasn't. He was at Ms. Nancy's house. Anna remembered a time when she and Angela were walking down this back street, which was Ninth St., hoping to see if their dad had made it home. Yes, they only lived several blocks from each other. Picture this: the back road, which is Ninth St., was the street where all the criminals would dump their trash after their horrendous crimes that they wanted to keep hidden.

Angela noticed someone lying on the side of the road—she screamed and started running, and so did Anna. When they stopped running someone saw them and said, "That is a dead body," and the police were called. Anna and Angela didn't stick around. Anna knew that she couldn't keep going from house to house looking for her father. So, she didn't look any further. It was too much work trying to keep up with her father. She finally realized that she couldn't find him. How do you put out a missing person report on someone who is not missing?

All Anna wanted was her father's attention—just to be in his presence. So, she drew close to other things that were closer to home. *Enough is enough!*

LOOKING FOR LOVE IN ALL THE WRONG PLACES

Tina, Anna's oldest sister, realized that menstrual cramps were very painful for Anna. She offered pain medication with codeine to ease Anna's pain. Tina was Anna's "ace koon boon" (BFF); though she was her sister and nine years older than her, they were very close. Anna didn't know why, because Tina was always getting in trouble with their mother. That door to addiction was kicked wide open. She made sure that Anna would go to the doctor with her and never missed an appointment. Anna, at the time, was only fourteen years old. She was already struggling with abandonment, rejection, and sexual assault issues; now, addiction wanted to rear its ugly head. This addiction hit Anna with a vengeance! As an infant, she had been on pain medication due to the trauma she had experienced in her mother's womb.

Anna's body jumped into taking medicine as if it were an old friend—well, it was; she had endured many surgeries as an infant. Anna's mother had told her that one time when she was in so much pain and it wasn't time for her medicine, Anna bit her—and she was tired of her biting, so she bit back, and after that she never bit her or anyone else! She felt that Anna was in pain and needed someone to know how bad it was for her. Anna's painkiller intake grew more and more. It was a way to numb the pain. She knew deep down inside that something wasn't right with this picture, but she had a void, and pills filled the void. What was she thinking? She wasn't.

She was not in her right mind! This journey worsened because of the choices she made. *Momma and Daddy, I need you so much*, was Anna's cry. Her mother was there, the best that she could be. No matter how hard her mother tried, they still saw the pain in her eyes. Anna realized that she could no longer make her laugh. Her mother was in and out of hospitals. Anna was the oldest sibling at home now, but the sad thing was that Anna couldn't help her mother, nor her family. Anna's younger brother had this bully at school. Her brother was what you would call a nerd, a bookworm, an honor roll student. He was a target for those who weren't. Anna walked into the cafeteria, and this boy was bullying her little brother. Reginald was sitting there, taking it. Well, here came Anna to the rescue. "Boy, you'd better leave my brother alone, or you're going to wish you had!" Anna was wrong for threatening him. She knew that she wasn't going to do anything.

Little did Anna know that this boy had a big sister named Margaret, who looked like "the Terminator," with three notorious (big) friends who were crazier than Margaret. Well, after school, Anna got the great beat down by all four of them, and they injured her eardrum. Anna couldn't help herself! Why was she trying to help her brother? He was bigger than Anna. Love had made her do it! Anna's mother never knew what all had happened, because Anna couldn't tell her; she didn't want her to be hurt more than what she already had been. Now it would have been Anna that had hurt her mother. *Enough is enough*!

Anna's mother would always say, "You'd better not get pregnant!" So, what did Anna do? She got pregnant—not intentionally, of course! Anna's friends had told her it couldn't happen on the first time *Dah*! At the age of sixteen, she gave birth to her son, Damion. She wasn't ready to be a mother, and abortion wasn't an option. Anna knew that she would love her child like she had never known love before! She was not ready to be a mother in high school, so she had to go to night school. Anna was still carrying the past like a monkey on her back that wouldn't let go. His daddy, Tyrone, at first said it wasn't his, but he realized soon that it was. There were no others—just the two that had raped her, which was years prior. She thanked God that she hadn't started her period yet then, or that could have been a bigger problem. She realized that she had to grow up and do it quick, so she married him and moved into their place. Anna was still looking for her Father!

Anna knew that Tyrone was not good for her. There was a time when Anna was sitting in the car with a church friend at her mom's home, who had brought her home from church; he was telling her that she needed to get out that relationship. Out of nowhere Tyrone pulled up, and he busted the guys' window out, snatched Anna out of the car, and commenced to beating her. Of course, that guy ran. Anna tried to run too, but when he caught her, it got worse!

As Anna was running, she picked up a bottle, threw it, and broke Tyrone's car window. She wasn't trying to hit his car. She just wanted Tyron to stop. Tyrone caught Anna, opened his rear car door, and pushed her into the seat where all the glass was. Anna was forced into the glass; her rear end was cut in numerous places. Anna went to the hospital that day and got the glass removed—her ankle was also sprained—and she was released. The sad thing was that Anna thought it was her fault. Anna should've ended this then, but she didn't. Anna didn't know who she was, and being raped at nine and twelve years of age didn't help any. Some statements aren't good, no matter how good they sound.

"I spank you because I love you! I cause you pain because I love you!" We know that this was not the intent of the statement, but I'm sure some of us heard it. I'm sure he had heard it as well, growing up. That's probably where he found that line. Tyrone said, "I love you, and I didn't want anyone else to have you." That sounds romantic; well, it's not!

That's abuse, and that's all it is. Don't be deceived—this is not love! Tyrone pleaded, said he loved her, and that it would never happen again. That was a lie from the pit of hell, and she believed that lie. Please get out of this, Anna! No one told her that she deserved better. No one told her that she deserved to be loved. Anna was teaching him how to treat her, so it got worse. **Enough is enough**!

There was still that void; at that time, she still couldn't understand it. She didn't know why it was like she had a stamp on her forehead that said, "Hurt me!" She married Tyrone at the age of eighteen. They both came from abusive families, and her mother told her not to do it. Love has a name when you put your heart in the wrong hands. She thought *hardhead* and *stupid*! She was stuck on *stupid*! Anna calling herself stupid sounds so harsh—she was deceived and blinded by what she thought was love. Anna was so determined to give her son what she never had—a father in the home—so she ignored her mother. She was repeating her mother's life and didn't see it! A man being in the house makes him a father no more than a Pinto being in the garage makes it a Cadillac.

A couple of months after Anna and Tyrone were married, he went to prison for two years for armed robbery. He stated that it wasn't him, but she was sure that the four times he had gone to jail before wasn't him either, just wrong identity. She was relieved when he went to prison, because Anna was tired of him hurting her. Anna knew when she got home what would happen. She wasn't any better—remember, she had sworn that no man would hurt her again.

That vow she had made to herself, which she didn't keep, only made her a woman with a big mouth! Her kids heard her mouth crying, arguing, or singing to forget the pain. It was so dysfunctional for her children to live in that atmosphere, but Anna didn't know that. That mouth made matters worse for her. Anna didn't know when to shut up! The weird thing was that they had known each other as kids through their fathers, and then they had met in high school. For some reason, Anna thought it was destiny. She began to wish that destiny would shut up!

Anna realized quickly that it was destiny for her to get a divorce while Tyrone was still in prison. She was hoping to have it completed before he got out. He had told Anna numerous times that he would kill her before he would see her with someone else. He meant every word of it! Anna believed him but was so naïve.

DANGER—ALERT, ALERT!

A woman Anna knew from the apartment complex she lived in talked her into going out one night, so she did. She figured, what's the harm in that? Anna was still new to being out of her mother's house, and her soon-to-be ex-husband was still away, so why not? She took Anna to a club called the Regal Room. Anna believed that she could trust her, since she knew where she lived. Can you trust anybody? Often Anna wondered, was she a magnet for trouble, or naïve, or was she not aware of a hit out on her life?

The woman and Anna got to the club. They were having a good time, and she introduced Anna to her "Cuz." I did say that Anna was naïve—Cuz (cousin) was a name people called someone they had only seen a time or two when they forgot a person's name. Seriously, Anna thought it was her cousin. So, it was time for the club to close, and she wasn't leaving with a guy she had just met. Of course, Anna had left her car at home since the woman was driving. She said, "Anna, Cuz likes you, and he will drop you off at home." Anna told her that she didn't know him, and she said, "He's good people, girl; it's cool!" Instantly, Anna had that feeling come over her.

She didn't know what it was. So, she got in the car with him. He lived in St. Louis, and after he raped Anna, he put her out of the car on a bridge and said, "Walk home!" Anna picked up the pieces again and walked home! *Enough is enough!*

The unthinkable had happened again. Anna had been raped for the third time. Anna started drinking and didn't want to live anymore. Anna took her son over to her mother's house, and she decided that this was it. Then Anna got back that morning to find her apartment burglarized. The thieves had violated her. They took her television, her telephone, and all the food in the refrigerator. She called the police; there was nothing they could do. Anna was so scared to stay in her apartment that night, so she went back to her mother's house. Strange as it is, that break-in saved her life! She'd had the liquor and the pills. The time at her mother's home gave her a new perspective. She realized how much she loved her son, and that he loved and needed her!

DADDY WAS LOST, BUT NOW FOUND

A couple of months after the break-in, Anna's father became ill and was hospitalized. She didn't need to look for him anymore. She finally knew where he was. After the death of her oldest brother, Skeeter, her father had blamed himself for his death so much that he started drinking heavily. Anna's father was an alcoholic, and his drinking had caused him to have cirrhosis of the liver. The woman he had loved so much—that Anna's mother had gone through hell for—put him out due to his drinking and womanizing. If they cheat with you, they will cheat on you! He began to sleep wherever else he could lay his head, including on the corner of any given street. Anna felt sorry for her Dad!

Anna remembered the day when she, her brother David, and her sister Angela (Ms. Martha's kids by her father) were walking home after school. When they arrived at the corner where Blackmon's Liquor Store was located on Ninth St., there was their Daddy, passed out drunk. David and Angela started making fun of him. Anna got so mad that she started crying and wanted to fight them. How could they talk about him like that when he gave up everything to be with them? The way Anna talked made them feel so bad that the three gathered what money they could, which wasn't much, and bought some chips out of the store so he could eat.

The very family that Anna's father had wanted so badly was now embarrassed by him. This handsome, tall, sharp-dressed man she remembered didn't look the same anymore. Her Daddy was considered another bum on the street, which is what others called him. Anna always hated people making fun of other people. The urban dictionary defines *bum* as, "usually a homeless person with a chronic addiction to alcohol and/or street drugs, with possible mental health issues, no care about appearance or personal hygiene, and having little to no respect for themselves." The doctors had warned him over the years that he must stop drinking, but he didn't—he couldn't. Alcoholism is a sickness, a disease! Her father's past had caught up with him—the children's lives, his abuse of a woman who loved him, the heartache that other women suffered, the abuse he did to his body, and not being there when his oldest son needed him. All he needed to do was to accept help, but he couldn't, or he wouldn't. ***Enough is enough***!

It was now October 1981; Anna went to the hospital to see him before he died. He was so thin, and his stomach was swollen. He was in a coma. She never got the chance to say goodbye, or, "I loved you, no matter what." He never said he was sorry, and she never remembered him ever saying he loved her. The family was informed that he had accepted the Lord Jesus Christ as his Savior before he died. Daddy was gone! She was so thankful that he had accepted Christ as his

Lord and Savior, but what would have happened if he had said, "Yes, Lord!" years before? Anna no longer needed to look for her father. She could finally let him go, right along with the pain, and find forgiveness.

Anna's mother was truly the greatest women who had ever lived, because after everything she went through with him and these women, she remained humble. Her mother was a woman of grace and dignity. Though she cried, she held her head up high. Though the other women and their children were there at the funeral, she greeted them as if they were her friends. Anna watched her mother so she could see what would happen. It was the Spirit of the Lord upon her mother. God had given her the grace to endure!

After the third sexual assault, someone breaking into her apartment, and losing the man she had been chasing for over twenty-two years (her daddy), Anna had had all that she could stand. Her neighbor wasn't a friend at all. After Anna's apartment was burglarized, she became very distant. Anna realized that that woman and Cuz had set her up that night at the club. Anna was so naïve—though she had lived in East St. Louis, she had refused to let East St. Louis live in her! Anna was in it, but she wasn't of it. She refused to hate people, though they hated her. ***Enough is enough***!

A BEAUTIFUL GIFT THAT'S

COMPLICATED

She thought that moving from that area was a new beginning—but moving somewhere with the same monkey on her back didn't stop the show. Anna was still waiting on the courts to dissolve her marriage to Tyrone, hopefully before he got out of prison. A couple of months before Tyrone got out, Anna met a man named Clayton. He was nice and had been reared in a Christian home. Though Clayton's mother was a praying Christian woman, he lived contrary to what he knew to be the truth. They became very fond of each other, and he knew that she had filed for a divorce. One night—which is all it takes—they went too far without protection.

One night, Anna went with her sister Carolyn to see her husband perform at a jazz club in St. Louis. After the show, they went to White Castle. She loved their food. Anna decided to run in and get the food, since her sister was doing the driving, and run right back out. Right—it sounded good. While Anna was second in line, suddenly everything went black. She was out for the count! Anna had passed out. When Anna woke up, she saw a white lady standing over her, which was rare in that area. Anna thought, *What in the world happened?* The lady asked Anna, "Are you all right? Do you know where you are? You are in White Castle, and you fainted!" "Yes, I'm all right, just embarrassed!" Anna said. She tried to stand up and couldn't. She knew that she didn't drink anything, because her stomach was already upset. Carolyn ran in, got Anna, and took her home. Oh no, what now?

The next day, Anna found out that she was pregnant. "What have I done? I'm on birth control—this can't be," she cried. "I'm pregnant, and I'm married to a man who will be released from prison soon. He is going to kill me!" Anna cried. Anna still hadn't legalized the divorce. They were telling her to fill out the papers again. At this point, she was terrified! Anna wrote to Tyrone in prison so it wouldn't be such a shock when he got out. Everyone was telling Anna to get an abortion. That never crossed Anna's mind, because she'd had this dream, and the dream had informed her that this was the little girl she'd always wanted. On top of this, Tyrone was released from prison early and showed up on her doorstep like, "Honey, I'm home!" Clayton was there, but not like that—Clayton was trying to talk Anna into not taking Tyrone back.

Anna was telling Clayton how Tyrone was, and that he would hurt him. She had to stop seeing Clayton until everything was final. Anna never should've opened that door. The story of her life—too many open doors, and all of them leading to destruction. Well, Tyrone and Clayton got into a fight! Anna was pregnant and trying to stop them. Tyrone threw Clayton out, telling him that Anna was his wife, and no one would ever have her! She was scared straight—straight into taking this man back. You know a person has a problem when their family says they have a problem—believe them! It was either that or die. Did she hear someone say, "Call the police"?

In East St. Louis in the eighties, you needed to call the police on the police—if you could find one that wasn't dirty and that cared. By the way, she tried that. Her husband was smart. If he didn't leave bruises, which were proof, they wouldn't even take a report. What law? She was sleeping with the enemy. People stay in domestic violence situations for several reasons. Just a few: they love that person, thinking that they must love them because they don't want anyone else to have them; financial stability; or staying out of fear for their life. Anna had mistaken control for love! For Anna, fear was a reality, especially if she left him or wasn't where she was supposed to be.

One day Anna's car broke down; it was so hot, and there were no cell phones back then. Who pulled up? Clayton. She was pregnant and hot, and he offered her a ride to her mother's house, only a few blocks away. What in the world was she thinking? Tyrone was always somewhere lurking, or else she had the worst timing imaginable. As soon as she got out of the car, Tyrone sped up—not drove up, sped up! All she was thinking was, *Momma, be home!* He snatched her, threw her down to the ground, and then there was a gun up to her head. She was screaming, but no one was coming. Clayton was nowhere to be seen; he had burnt out. Suddenly, Anna heard the gun go off! It was just a few inches from her head! Tyrone said, "I'll kill you!"

He removed the gun from her head. She was shaking so badly. All she could think about was her baby. She grabbed her stomach to make sure that her baby was okay. All that day she spent trying to think of ways to get out of this. Yet she could still hear his voice saying, "I'll kill you! If you leave me, I'll kill you!" No one owns anyone! *Enough is enough*!

After Clayton had burnt out, leaving Anna lying on the ground pregnant with his daughter, with a gun up to her head—and he didn't even call for help—Anna realized that she had no one she could count on, no one she could trust. After her daughter Albany was born, Tyrone became her father. She looked more like him than she did Anna, even to this day. Albany loved her father, Tyrone, and you couldn't say anything bad about him to her. Tyrone could do no wrong, even if she saw it—and they did. He spoiled her. Anna could say one thing: he took care of his children. When things were good, they were good! But Anna knew that she couldn't just act like Clayton and his family didn't exist.

Anna would sneak Albany to see Clayton's family, even if she would've been caught doing it. Anna was beaten on numerous occasions after leaving Albany's grandmother's home, but Tyrone never knew where she was. She never told Albany who her grandmother was, because Albany would tell Tyrone. They could never say that Anna didn't bring Albany to see them, though some of them wouldn't show up for a visit, being angry with her. Anna understood their anger, but if they only knew what it took to get her there. Clayton's mother loved the visits; seeing her face when she saw Albany was always worth the pain, the fights, and the fear of what would happen if he found out. For a season, the abuse stopped, but the adultery increased. It was the beginning of bitterness!

Anna's heart had become so bitter. She would think of ways she could get out of this marriage—one way or the other! Drugs had become a big part of their lives, but their children didn't go without anything, except the full attention of their parents—sounds familiar. A repeated dysfunctional family cycle. One time her oldest sister Tina said, "The only way you will get out of this marriage is if one of you dies!" Tina, please don't give Anna any ideas! Interestingly enough, that is why Tina and Tyrone hated each other so much.

CHAPTER 3

ALL IN THE FAMILY

FAMILY DINNER

Anna's house was the place to be. Her family knew: if they were hungry, go to Anna's; in trouble, go to Anna's; weekends and holidays, go to Anna's! Yes, she was from the south—Anna could cook; where she found peace was in her kitchen. What's weird is that no one would bother her there. Tyrone wasn't going to stop dinner from being prepared! She remembered "Famous Fish Fry Friday"; everybody was there. One night it was getting late, and her baby brother Tyrone (Ty) wanted to hang out longer; before she knew it, she said to him, "I don't know where in the world you are going, but you are going to get the heck out of here!" Ty looked at her and yelled, "You have become a ('B' word)!" That word cut her to her core. She was stunned that he had called her that. He was right, and it was the truth! What happened to you, Anna? Anna had become consumed with bitterness, pain, and regret. Now, this was her baby brother. They were very close. But Anna had changed. She didn't care about anything anymore. Anna was broken and bitter to the root.

Their relationship had been very close. Years prior, Anna had had a dream about her brother Ty. He was out late one night and was in trouble. Anna was at home, sound asleep.

She woke up screaming, "My leg!" Her left leg had this sharp pain in it. It was a pain that Anna had never felt before. At the same time, Ty called her and said, "Anna, I've been shot in the leg!" It was the same leg. She had felt his pain! That is how close they had been, but Anna had changed. The bitterness was eating away at her. A life of sexual assaults and physical and mental abuse was taking its toll on her. It had hardened her heart. *Enough is enough*!

MOMMA, WHERE ART THOU?

The bitterness was affecting every area of her life: physical, mental, and social. The stress in her life had caused her to start having female issues. She was now like the woman with the issue of blood. The doctors had decided that she would need a partial hysterectomy. She started talking to her mother about it because Anna was afraid. Anna didn't know anything about female issues, and she needed her mother to tell her what to do. Anna and her mother went to the same doctor, and they happened to show up at the same time. Anna's mother was waiting on the pharmacist to fill her medication, and she began to say to her mother, "Momma, I'm scared! I don't want to go through this surgery, Momma!" Her mother's favorite phrase for everything was, "Baby, just trust in the Lord!" Anna said, "Momma, I need more than that!"

"The surgery is scheduled for January 15, Momma!" Anna said. "Trust him, Anna Jean!" said Momma. "Okay, Momma, but you have got to be there, or I will not have this surgery." "Don't worry, Anna Jean!" said Momma. "I can take you home, Momma," said Anna. Momma said, "I already have a car on the way to pick me up, Anna." Anna asked, "Are you sure, Momma?" "Yes, I'm still waiting on my medicine," Momma replied. "Okay, Momma!" Anna got in her car and drove off. When her mother got home later that night, she had a massive heart attack. Anna got a call that she was at the hospital, in intensive care. "I was just with her! She can't be in the hospital. What's wrong with Momma?" Anna cried.

They went to the hospital, and her mother was helicoptered to another facility for heart surgery. Anna got there just in time to tell her mother, "I love you, and I'm sorry for upsetting you about the surgery." She looked at Anna and said, "You didn't; it's going to be okay, Anna!" Anna said, "Momma, please, you got to be okay!" That was the last time Anna spoke to her mom, and the last time she heard her voice. They put her on the helicopter; by the time Anna got to the other hospital, she was in surgery. Anna's mother came out of surgery but was in a coma. On December 27, a decision was made to unhook the life support. She was gone. Anna's mother was gone, just like that!

WHAT IN THE WORLD?

The night before the funeral, Anna was robbed of the opportunity to prepare for her mother's funeral in peace. Anna and her sister-in-law, Karen, were up late getting everything ready for the kids: their clothes, Damion's haircut, and Albany's hair fixed. The kids were exhausted, and Anna was still in shock. I don't have to tell you what was on her mind: Anna began to believe that everything bad that had happened was because she had caused it. This was a lie from the pit of hell! Anna had had nothing to do with her mother's death, but it took Anna years to accept this.

Anna's mind was racing ninety miles an hour, and she got home to drama. Now, she had to face Tyrone, who wanted to fight about why she was so late coming home. Anna said, "Are you kidding me? This not happening!" She went off, and so did he. He jumped on her—and to keep this part of the story short, she had to go to her mother's funeral with a huge bruise under her eye. Anna and Karen tried to cover it up with make-up, but it didn't work. This bruise was deeper than any wound she had ever had. "Tyrone, you robbed me," cried Anna.

At the funeral, the whole time while she was on the front row looking at her mother in that casket, she couldn't stop thinking about what Tyrone had done. Anna's heart was shattered into pieces, her body was agonized with pain, and her mind was wishing that Tyrone was in that casket instead of her mother. She had better cover these bruises up before Anna's uncles saw them! She was overwhelmed with pain. She could still see him throwing her against the wall. Once she hit the floor, then came his feet, stomping her. That night he had even started fighting Karen, his sister-in-law, as she had tried to explain.

Anna was in shock and didn't even know it. Anna continued to look around the room, thinking that they didn't even know what had happened—or about the time he had snatched her off the bus with the kids, or at the gas station getting gas, or on the corner of any given block! Trauma, denial, grief, anger, and pain consumed her. There are no words to describe what that day was like for her. Anna realized, as she sat there watching her mother, how she had suffered her whole life and it had ended in pain. Anna asked God as the preacher was preaching, "Is this my future, too?" Too much pain! *Enough is enough!*

Anna looked around the room. She could see people weeping, crying out, their lips moving; but she heard no sound. It was as if Anna was going through the motions. It felt as if everything was standing still. Anna wanted to scream at the top of her lungs, but she couldn't. She was at her mother's funeral and consumed with unbearable pain. It was the last time she would get to see her face. Anna kept thinking, *Don't leave me here! I want to go with you; don't leave me, Momma! I need you so bad!* Tyrone had robbed Anna of a day that she would never get again. It was time to go home and try to move forward, whatever that meant. Anna had been pushed over the edge. Enough is enough! Stop the violence! **Enough is enough!**

Anna and her daughter Albany went to the store a couple of days after the funeral. Anna was talking to the clerk, and suddenly, her speech slurred. It got worse—she couldn't talk. The only thing that came out made no sense. Anna couldn't form a full word without slurring or stuttering. She went to the hospital; the doctors thought she'd had a stroke. It wasn't a stroke, but the hospital kept Anna for three weeks. She had lost it; she was diagnosed with a breakdown. The time in the hospital was good. Anna had no distractions. There was only a bed and a nightstand in the room she was in, so she could focus on healing the pain and the grief that had consumed her.

It allowed her to finally focus on the pain of losing her mother, the pain she had endured through domestic violence, and the loss of her virginity and identity after the sexual assaults. Anna knew deep down inside that this was not her future. She always knew that there was something or someone calling her closer, though she didn't know what to do with those feelings. When Anna got home, she still couldn't speak without slurs, and it was thanks to her daughter Albany that she was able to communicate with people in public. The doctors had her on medication that she refused to take because it made her drowsy.

Anna's mother had always kept telling her to trust God. "Trust in the Lord, Anna!" Well, when her mother died, the surgery never took place. For nine years she had been on birth control to help with the issue of blood that constantly overflowed monthly. A routine follow-up visit to Dr. Adams informed her that she was pregnant. Anna said to Dr. Adams, "This can't be; there is no way that I'm pregnant." Albany was now nine years old. It dawned on Anna that if her mother had lived, the surgery would have taken place. There would never have been a Tyrone Jr. Sometimes she felt that her momma had died so that Tyrone Jr. (Lil Ty) could live. Anna wasn't supposed to have any more kids. Anna's womb was supposed to be too weak to carry another child due to the abuse. Lil Ty wasn't supposed to be here, but God! *I am the God who sees!*

The birth of Lil Ty almost killed her; when she left the hospital from having surgery with him, the State of Illinois healthcare ordered a live-in nurse. Her name was Mrs. Black. Yes, Anna was that sick! Anna was having severe pain in her head from the epidural shot they had injected into her spine for the C-section. Anna couldn't take care of her children nor herself; the nurse had to help her do everything. She couldn't get out of bed without screaming in pain. Anna would scream for dear mercy. Anna wanted to die. If she'd had a gun, she would've blown her head off. God sent that nurse. She ministered to Anna the Word of God. It was a setup!

GOD SET IT OFF!

The nurse prayed for Anna, encouraged her, and spoke life into her. Tyrone had moved to Colorado to look for a place to send for her and the kids, promising a new beginning that would end the abuse. She thought this was her way of escape, but the nurse said, "Go; leave this place and don't look back!" Anna told her, "I need to leave him." Mrs. Black said, "I know, but God wants you there!" She said, "It is different there; he will not be able to abuse you, and if he does, call the police— they will help you. If you can make it here, you can make it anywhere!"

Anna moved to Colorado with Tyrone. She had to focus on getting her children out of East St. Louis. Anna needed her children to have a different view of life than what she had seen. Anna was sleeping with the enemy of Tyrone's soul and warring against the enemy who wanted to take her soul. Tyrone continued to commit adultery; while he was chasing those women, Anna was chasing God! She knew she needed deliverance. She was damaged, but not forsaken by God. What Anna could see was hope, and it looked better than what she had endured for the last sixteen years. Anna finally jumped into God's arms! "God will be with me," said Anna. Anna was seeking Jesus, and everything would be all right now, so they said. For God is the God who sees!

HAVE MERCY, LORD; WHAT NOW?

Three months after Anna moved to Colorado, when Lil Ty was six months old, Damion, her older son, began to rebel at the age of fifteen. He hadn't wanted to move to Colorado. Damion had lost his grandmother. After losing her, they had moved to Colorado, and then he lost his grandfather. One night, Damion was due to go to court the next day; he had committed a crime, but he didn't want to go to jail. A parent's nightmare is when their child begins to hang out with the wrong people. Gang members had become his friends. Damion had come into the house, scared about what the next day would bring. He and Anna talked, and she said, "It's going to be okay! I will be with you, Damion!" She told him, "I will ask the judge to have mercy on you, and tell him that you've never done this before, and you will never do this again." "I can't go to jail, Momma," said Damion.

Albany, Lil Ty, and Anna were watching TV. Everything was calm and quiet. Suddenly, Anna heard a loud sound coming from the basement. She ran to the top of the steps. She called out to Damion, "What was that?" Damion began to walk up the steps, holding his stomach in agony. Anna said, "What's wrong?" He made it up the steps. She was holding him, not knowing he had just shot himself! Anna ran to the phone to call 911. She was running back and forth from Damion to the phone. Damion made it to her room and collapsed at the door. She dropped the phone to go to him. She checked to see what was wrong with his stomach. He had shot himself!

There was a hole in his stomach—no blood, just a hole. Tears were falling from his eyes while looking into her eyes. "My baby, what have you done?" asked Anna. The operator was still on the phone, trying to remain calm. Albany and Lil Ty were crying. The operator was asking questions to help Anna get the police there. Anna had to pull it together. Anna couldn't fall apart! Everything horrific she had ever been through had brought her to this moment. She sent Albany and Lil Ty to their room. The operator was telling Anna, "Don't hang up the phone; help is on the way." The ambulance arrived. "Help my baby!" Anna cried.

After what felt like forever to Anna, help finally arrived. There were numerous police and ambulance lights and sirens. They rushed in and grabbed her son, put him on the gurney, and off to the hospital he went. The police ran up the steps from the basement with a gun—a black gun that Anna had never seen before. They had never had a gun in their home. Damion had hidden it behind the sofa in his room. Suddenly, handcuffs were put on Anna! "What is going on?" she screamed. "I got to get to my son. My son!" Anna screamed.

It was September 21, which was a very cold night in Colorado. Her children were scared and crying. Anna was forced out of the door of her home by the police and led to a paddy wagon. Anna's neighbor looked out the door and said, "Where are your kids?" Anna replied, "In the house—please get them!" Diane got the children. Anna was walking down the sidewalk with handcuffs on, in shorts and a t-shirt and house shoes! She was in shock! She kept telling them, "I got to get to my son."

They put gloves on Anna's hands, which would collect gun residue. She was crying, "I didn't shoot my son! What are you doing?" The test was negative. She was standing in the cold, begging them to take her to her son. They had thought that Anna had shot her son because she had dropped the phone to take care of her him while on the phone with the operator. She was finally allowed to go to her son!

Anna changed clothes, and the police took her to her son. She got to the hospital and he was in intensive care. "Lord, I need you! My son needs you," Anna cried out. "Spare his life, Lord!" Anna had previously lost a nephew to suicide; her faith was on trial. Tyrone and his family were at the hospital when she got there. The bullet had traveled through the inside, tearing up his intestines. There were many tubes hooked to him. The doctors were telling her, "It's not good. If he lives, he will be using a colostomy bag for the rest of his life." God spared Anna's son's life after three weeks in intensive care. Anna cried, "Thank you, Jesus, for hearing my cry!" But God!

Finally, Anna's son was released from intensive care with a colostomy bag. The doctors told Anna, "Your son will never have any children, and he will be on a colostomy bag for the rest of his life." She had to stay focused on being there for him. The God whom she was learning more and more about had to help her with her faith. Damion came home, and Anna nursed her son back to health by the grace of God. The hospital taught Anna how to clean his wounds because his stomach couldn't be stitched up; it had to heal from the inside out. She was taught how to change/empty the colostomy bag. Anna would sing, pray, and speak the Word over Damion morning, noon, and night.

God did it! Damion's colostomy bag was removed. He no longer needed it. Why couldn't Anna have seen the pain her son was in due to leaving their home? Damion hadn't wanted to leave their family. He had lost his grandmother, who was Anna's mom, and he was hurting. Anna, being wrapped up in her pain, didn't see his. Our children are suffering, and we don't see it. **Enough is enough**! God sees!

THE LAST FIGHT

Anna had to realize that she wasn't focused on her children like other mothers were. Anna was broken. Tyrone fought Anna one last time; this time he broke her tailbone in two. Enough was enough! The movie *Waiting to Exhale* had just come out. Something changed in her when she saw it. She began to pray one thing: *save* him or *move* him! God did it! Tyrone moved out and got engaged. Anna finally dared to get her divorce. This divorce was sixteen years past due. Honestly, it had been eighteen years of abuse. What was she thinking, blindsided by her love and fear? She never looked back at what broke her. God made sure of that. **Enough is enough**!

Anna realized that she couldn't just blame him. Anna had sworn that no one would ever treat her like her father had treated her mother. I guess the enemy was saying, "You want to bet?" Her mouth got her into trouble a lot. Anna was a hot mess—toxic, broken, shattered, beaten, and battered, and in need of healing. She stopped blaming others and began to blame herself. It was no longer outward; it was inward. The enemy—inner me! On the day of the divorce, Anna got so drunk that she passed out. The kids were at their dad's house for the weekend. When she woke up, she was on her kitchen floor.

Anna had finally hit rock bottom. One day, Anna came home from work and turned on the television, and this apostle was preaching—she knew it was a word from the Lord. Anna went to visit Now Faith Christian Center Church in Denver, and Apostle Emerson prophesied that her life had been pure hell, but that God was restoring her. Anna had finally found her Father—God!

Anna got baptized during the Sunday night service, and she came up speaking in a heavenly language. A language she did not learn, but which was a gift from God. His Spirit descended on Anna like a dove. Later, after the baptism in the service, as she was praising God, everything went pitch black. Anna was no longer in the service; she was there, but not there. It felt like it had gone on forever, but it was only a few minutes! When she came out of it, her clothes were soaked and wet. Anna was "tore up from the floor up." As she was coming out of it, she could hear Apostle Emerson saying, "Have your way, God, have your way!" Anna felt like Saul, who was blinded on the road to Damascus by Jesus. Anna had never persecuted anyone, especially not Christians. She might have been through hell, but she wasn't crazy. Saul had received his sight again, and he had become Paul! God had to knock her out—literally. A spiritual TKO! *I am the God who sees!*

CHAPTER 4

TRANSFORMED INTO HIS IMAGE

And be not conformed to this world: but be ye transformed by the renewing of your mind, that ye may prove what is that good, and acceptable, and perfect, will of God.

Romans 12:2

Anna found Love's Way! Love knew exactly where Anna was, though Anna didn't know Him. Anna was becoming more like Christ! The Lord Jesus began to remove the yokes of bondage off of her from her past. Anna's mind began to be renewed by seeking His face in prayer, studying His Word, and fasting. She became desperate. She had never wanted help more than she did the day that she was predestined to run into that church. Anna couldn't take any more of herself. She began to understand the words, "I will!" *Enough is enough!*

Anna surrendered. "Whatever you want me to do, I'll do! I'll pray, I'll sing, I'll fast; I will!" God's love was consuming Anna. Anna had to forgive everyone that had hurt her Yes, all those who had raped, molested, abused, and stolen from her were forgiven, because she wanted forgiveness. Anna had read in the Bible, in Matthew 6:14-15 (KJV), "For if ye forgive men their trespasses, your heavenly Father will also forgive you: But if ye forgive not men their trespasses, neither will your Father forgive your trespasses." Anna had felt justified in holding onto that hatred for them, but it was eating away at the core of her. She came to understand that of them to whom much is given, much is required. God had forgiven her for much, so it was required for her to forgive them. No, it wasn't easy—it was one of the hardest things she had ever had to do! She began to pray for them. It is hard to pray for someone who has hurt you! You just had to keep doing it until it just happened, and then it was so. Love filled her because He is the God who sees!

Anna began to work in the ministry. She was on the usher board, was youth usher leader, and occasionally served in the hospitality ministry. She wanted to be available to do and be everything that God wanted her to do and be. She would show up before the doors of the church opened for prayer meetings, including Sunday school. For three years, all she wanted was Jesus. Jesus was her husband now, and that was all she needed. She was free, loved, and a part of a family that felt the same way that she did. Well, at least that's what she thought; but everything isn't always what it seems. Anna should have let her Father God lead and guide her.

CONFIRM, CONFIRM, CONFIRM

One Sunday night service, a preacher was preaching a powerful message. The title was, "You Need Not Fight in This Battle!" She had seen him numerous times, yet not seen him. She had just been divorced two years prior, so she didn't allow herself to see men. No disrespect—she needed to continue to heal, and she had too much baggage. When she got her divorce, it was just her and her children.

Anna didn't have family or friends in Colorado other than

those she had met in her church, and her ex-husband's family had an obligation to him and his new wife. He would get the kids on the weekend—which was an additional problem, because Anna was trying to raise the children in a Christian household, but on weekends they lived a different lifestyle. Hanging out at clubs with their dad, seeing the life he was living, and desiring it at any cost. Anna still had to thank God that He provided for His children, and God protected them from any harm.

See, Anna was still a new Christian (a babe in Christ) and didn't know what all was in the church. She had become a Martha when she should have been more like Mary. See, Martha in Luke 10 was distracted with much serving. "And she went up to him (Jesus) and said, 'Lord, do you not care that my sister has left me to serve alone? Tell her then to help me.' But the Lord answered her, 'Martha, Martha, you are anxious and troubled about many things, but one thing is necessary. Mary has chosen the good portion, which will not be taken from her'" (Luke 10:40-42 ESV). See, Anna should have been more in the Word of God instead of working so much. Anna should have been more at the feet of Jesus instead of serving, thinking she needed to work for her salvation. Not so, being saved by grace (unmerited favor) and having been already paid for by the blood of Jesus! All she had to do was believe and receive. When you try to work for your own salvation, you are under the law! Mary was getting to know Him in the process of developing a relationship between them by sitting at His feet. This eternal life is an intimate relationship with God the Father, God the Son, Jesus, and God the Holy Spirit. Intimacy is getting to know God! Anna hadn't gotten the chance to know God; her mind had not even been renewed. All she knew was to stay in the house!

Anna was so happy to be saved! Once she got in the house (church), she said, "*I'm staying in the house!*" She just wanted to please God. Anna missed a good portion of the preached Word. You need the preached Word, prayer, and your study time in the Word of God (the Bible) to be able to know how to divide the Word rightly. It is written in 2 Timothy 2:15 (KJV), "Study to shew thyself approved unto God, a workman that needeth not to be ashamed, rightly dividing the word of truth."

The Bible lets us know that there will be wheat and tares, and to let them grow together (Matthew 13:30). Anna learned something the hard way: that everyone who says "Lord, Lord," isn't saved. Sitting in the church doesn't make a person a Christian (a Spirit-filled/led believer). It's important to know that a person has the Holy Spirit! More importantly, does the Holy Spirit have them? Is the fruit of the Spirit operating in their life? Allow the Word of God to transform you! *Enough is enough!*

A UNION OF TWO DAMAGED PEOPLE

After one of the Sunday night services, Minister Mitch got Anna's attention to say hi. She thought that was nice of him. Eventually, the "hi" became long conversations after church. Sometimes they would talk about church events and the rearing of their children as single parents. Minister Mitch eventually asked her for her phone number, it was given, and then came the dates. Anna was trying to stay focused, but she figured she could use a friend. They had some things in common, as far as their children and church. Even with him being ten years older than she was, they were still able to talk about these things without confrontation or arguing. Then, it happened! He asked her the question after six months of just talking—yes, just talking! She didn't play that anymore. Hey, she had been there, done that, sad to say. Who wants to buy the cow if the milk is free?

"Would you marry me?" Now, this was the last thing on her

mind up until then. You must remember that her ex-husband had said, "No man will ever want her—a woman with three kids." Well, you can tell a person that for so long, they'll begin to believe you. So yes, that question was flattering. Maybe she didn't know at the time that she could have let her ex-husband know that he was wrong. She couldn't answer that question yet. At that time, she didn't have any idea of what the answer would be. She was praying to God to tell her what to do.

One Sunday night she went to their church service, and there was a visiting prophet who was prophesying over the members. The prophet was no one she had ever heard of before, and only a very few people in the church knew who he was. As Minister Mitch came into the service, he sat by her for the first time, and she was shocked—because previously, they hadn't wanted anyone to think more of their relationship than what it was. Even then, he didn't sit close. There is a discerning of spirits, and the prophet knew what was going on.

While they were sitting in the service, the prophet called them both up. The prophet looked at Anna and said, "Yes, wife!" She was in shock yet again, because she wasn't quite familiar with prophets or the spirit of prophecy. How did he know? *It must be God*, Anna thought. So, she said yes to Minister Mitch. Jesus said, in Matthew 18:16 (NKJV), "...by the mouth of two or three witnesses every word may be established." Jesus is here quoting Deuteronomy 19:15 (NKJV), "...by the mouth of two or three witnesses the matter shall be established." Anna hadn't read that scripture, nor did she know that God confirms His word. He hadn't told her yes; just the prophet had.

Well, she was in it now; she wasn't positive that she was supposed to marry him. There were things that he did before the marriage that didn't make sense, but she felt she must make it work. There was no physical attraction, but that didn't matter to Anna; she just wanted to do God's will according to the prophet. Minister Mitch was not a Tyrone—thank you, Jesus! He walked in authority that was spiritual, with no compassion—unless he wanted to impress you! Anna had learned from the first marriage to shut her mouth, but Anna went too far to the left this time. He was verbally abusive and was mean to her children. Even if she tried to tell him that was not right, she was convicted and surrendered to his authority as a husband and a minister. Anna was beginning to die spiritually, but God was always fighting for her! *Enough is enough! I am the God who sees!*

One day Anna was sick and praying in their bedroom, "Lord, show me your face!" She was crying out. Normally she would go into the bathroom to pray, so she wouldn't disturb her husband. She never made it there. The bedroom door was closed, and she didn't think he could hear her, because he was in the basement. Anna's voice would elevate when she was passionate about something. While she was praying, suddenly, the door flew open, and he was furious. He was fussing, his eyes were fire-red to the point that it scared her, and he went to take a step through the door; he couldn't put his foot down, so he reversed it. Anna still believes today that if he had made one step, that would have been his last one. In mid-sentence, he stopped fussing, turned around, and immediately went back to his office. Anna was like, "What just happened?" That man was never at a loss for words. Anna was reminded of the scripture 2 Chronicles 20:17 (NASB), "You need not fight in this battle." This battle is the Lord's!

One day, Lil Ty asked Minister Mitch if he liked kids. Anna was sitting right there with them. "Do you like kids, Mitch?" It took Mitch a while to answer, and then he said yes, but he didn't mean it. That weekend, Anna went to a women's conference, because at this time they were pastoring a church in Aurora, CO. Anna wanted to learn all she could about women in ministry. While Anna was away, she asked Minister Mitch to watch Lil Ty. She had already prepared everything Lil Ty needed for breakfast and lunch. All that was needed was to heat it and give it to him. Minister Mitch made Lil Ty stay in his room the whole day. Each time Lil Ty told Mitch he was hungry, he told him to shut up and stay in his room.

When Anna got home late that night, the first thing she did, of course, was to make sure that Lil Ty was good and had eaten all his food. To Anna's surprise, all the food still wrapped as she had left it. She called Lil Ty to see why he hadn't eaten his food. He said, "Mitch wouldn't let me come out of my room!" *What?* Lil Ty looked at his mother and said, "But it's okay. I stole a couple of pieces of bologna." *What?* Mitch told Anna that Lil Ty was getting on his last nerve. "*What?* Are you kidding me?"

OUT OF THE MOUTHS OF BABES

Anna never allowed him to keep Lil Ty again! Out of the mouths of babes. It was a day of complete craziness. Mitch was mad; Lil Ty was extremely bad for the umpteenth time at school; Albany was hanging out with her father at the motorcycle club and skipping school. It was all Anna could take. She picked up Lil Ty from school, and she was mad at him. Anna messed up and spanked (whipped) her son while being angry. She left a red mark on his butt. The next day Lil Ty went to school, and his butt was hurting. There happened to be a substitute nurse there who knew nothing about Anna as a parent, nor knew Lil Ty. Well, when Anna got to the school to pick up Lil Ty, she was greeted by the police and Children and Family Services. They stated, "We are here because we got a call on you for child abuse."

They said, "The nurse reported that Tyrone Jr. has a mark on his butt, and that you whipped him because he was bad."

All Anna could do was cry, "I am not a child abuser! I am a good mother!" Anna had to be honest—she should never have spanked him while she was angry. Lil Ty was released to go home with Anna an hour later. The police and Children and Family Services let it go, because they could see that this wasn't a case of abuse. Anna took parenting classes, because times have changed. Spare the rod and spoil the child—but she must be careful how she used it! Parents, we have been known to do this. Anna learned: don't spank your children when you are angry! Anna remembered her mother whipping her because the pharmacy had arrived at their home, and neither Anna nor Carolyn had opened the door. Anna's mother had needed that medication, and she was sick. Neither Anna nor Carolyn had wanted to answer the door, and they got in major trouble for it. They got their butts torn up! The times have changed, differences in wisdom and time. ***Enough is enough!***

Anna thanked God, because this could have been much worse! Albany came home after staying out late. An argument broke out between Anna and Albany, which happened often. Tyrone had spoiled Albany; every other word she spoke was, "Dad will do it; Dad will let me; Dad will buy it; Dad will get it!" Anna told her daughter Albany, "Tyrone can deal with this, because I'm not!" Anna told her to get out: "Go; you can be seventeen and grown at his house!" Huge mistake! Albany and Anna's relationship got worse.

Anna realized that she had thrown her daughter to the wolves for peace of mind. Lord, help us handle our children better than this! Times have changed. Anna cried all night long, night after night. She is still, to this day, apologizing, and has yet to be forgiven for the mistakes she made in the lives of her children. We do better when we know better! Anna finally forgave herself. We can't run our rebellious children into the arms of Satan and expect them to change for the better. Like Bishop Jakes says, "We run them off, then cry when they don't want anything to do with us!" Prayer changes things! *Enough is enough*!

Out of the mouths of babes—Lil Ty said to her, "You are letting Mitch squash you like a bug, Momma!" That marriage ended after seven years. She did a quitclaim deed on the home and gave it to him. Her home—valued at $200,000—was hers no more. Anna needed peace more than she needed a house. Mitch eventually lost the house. The same place where he wouldn't allow her to have peace, he couldn't keep. All Mitch said was, "Anna, you did nothing wrong!" What did that mean to Anna, once he had turned her life upside down? Anna went and found help from V2V Ministry in Colorado. At this point, there was a silent scream. Don't be ashamed to get help. Therapy is a way of releasing the pain from the trauma of abuse, sexual assault, and loss. This ministry gave Anna back her voice after the enemy had said, "You better not tell anyone! SSSHHHHH!" *Enough is enough*!

TO THE ROOT OF THE MATTER

After the divorce, Anna moved to Missouri. Anna had been born in St. Louis, but she moved to Florissant, which was one city over from Ferguson. She thought, *So many things keep happening; let me go back to the root of the matter!* The Lord ordered her steps (Psalm 37:23). Anna found a church home in Florissant, MO, called Faith Miracle Temple, where the "Glory Cloud" and the "Gold Dust" saturating the sanctuary was the norm. Anna witnessed so many miracles at FMT. The first time she had the pleasure of meeting with the pastor—now Bishop—at FMT, he looked her in the face and said, "You are safe here!" Anna would never forget that day!

Anna had never felt safe before, until that moment. Anna, over the years, had accumulated layers and layers of hurt, pain, low self-esteem, and trauma from the abuse. Deliverance is an ongoing process from layer to layer. In this house (God's house), she wasn't judged, wasn't manipulated, wasn't an outcast, and wasn't under a spirit of control or in bondage to fear. God is for the underdog: the wounded, abused, and ostracized. God is for you! He will never leave or forsake you!

He spoke to the woman in her—the one whose fears had bound her all of her life and the little girl that had been sexual assaulted. She was now in a safe place. She didn't know what that looked or felt like, but God was blessing Anna. She was able to buy another home. She loved her home, but she loved the Giver more! It had a huge backyard, yellow siding, a big, huge tree in the front yard, a red rose flower bed, three bedrooms, a full finished basement, and a family room. Anna believed, "This is God's gift for all the hell I have been through!" She held many family gatherings of BBQs and birthday parties. Anna was back with her family, restored, and home.

A couple of years after moving to Missouri, Anna lost a brother. Byron was Anna's father's youngest son by Ms. Martha. At that time, Anna hadn't seen this side of her family in several years. When Anna went back, her sister Angela had moved to Virginia. Anna's brother David had contracted HIV, her brother Gary had been found dead a couple of years earlier in California, and her sister Diana and their mother, Martha, had moved to Texas.

A cycle of deaths began to hit Anna's family. Anna's life was turned upside down, just when she thought, *Finally, some peace; how sweet it is!* No one was fussing, and she worked from home and could pray whenever she wanted. Hallelujah! Of course, this didn't last long. Before losing Gary, Ms. Martha had already lost her oldest daughter, Rochelle. Rochelle was an amazing woman of God who worked in ministry with her husband and their children. Rochelle just went to sleep one night and never woke up. She was the first to die in Ms. Martha's family. No one understood how or why she had passed away. It just didn't make sense. Her heart had just stopped beating. Anna had been in her teens when Rochelle had passed away. Then, a couple of years later, Ms. Martha had lost Michael. Michael was eighteen years old when he died. He was away at school, sitting in a park on a hill under a tree; he had just stopped to catch his breath. Michael never came down off that hill alive! Rochelle, Gary, Michael, and Byron— what happened? One minute you're here, and the next minute you're gone.

What was happening to Anna's siblings? Rochelle, Gary, Michael, and now Byron were gone—that's four children that Ms. Martha had lost. Anna's heart was broken! She remembered the good times at Ms. Martha's house. They had all hung out in the basement. Anna could still hear the laughter, joking, arguments, and fights. Anna and her siblings had set it off in that basement. Their house was fun, crazy, and wild. Anna was the only one who went to Ms. Martha's house out of her mother's children, and that was due to Anna's relationship with Angela. Angela and Anna were so close, as thick as thieves. The two got into a lot of trouble together. Angela could always talk Anna into doing things she wasn't supposed to do. Angela was brave; nothing scared her. She was a tomboy in her own right. Anna and Angela would go to their sister Diana's nightclub on a girl's night out. They were always in good hands, until they got home.

Angela and Anna both had to face abuse, which is called domestic violence. Anna remembered the bruises all over Angela's body. The black eyes, busted lip, and Angela's arm in a sling were becoming a typical lifestyle for them. No, they didn't enjoy it! How could they have allowed someone to treat them like that? They were sleeping with their own enemies, and they couldn't get out without consequences. Their lives were an example of what happens when a father or positive male figure is not around to show you how amazing, how beautiful, and how loved you are! *Enough is enough!*

Anna could talk to Angela about anything, and she kept it to herself. Anna never saw the abuse firsthand, but her oldest sister and brothers did. Angela never experienced the abuse of their dad and never knew that he was abusive. Their dad never beat Ms. Martha because he loved her and didn't want to lose her. Anna never understood why he treated her mother so horribly. Anna and her mother accepted that treatment, not knowing that you teach people how to treat and to love you. Anna had yet to understand that concept. The pain of losing someone you love hurts so much! Every death takes a piece of you with it!

UNTIL I SEE YOU AGAIN

Anna and Tina were very, close. Remember, Tina was Anna's oldest sister (same mom). Tina was a fighter and had no problem proving it. Anna always had to have her guard up because Tina didn't play. Someday Tina's story should be told, because she saw things Anna would never want to imagine— well, maybe not. Whenever Tina called, Anna went. When she said jump, Anna said, "How high?"

Anna received a call from Tina while she was at Thursday night Bible study at FMT, requesting her to come over to her house. This call was different. Tina sounded desperate to see Anna. Anna lived in Hazelwood, Missouri, which was a city over from Ferguson, and an hour away from East St. Louis, IL, where Tina lived. To go there at night was not a wise thing to do. Actually, it's insane! Anna asked Tyrone Jr. to go with her after church. "No, Momma," he said to Anna; he was afraid to go there at night also. Anna called Tina immediately after the service to let her know she couldn't come. Tina was persistent, but Anna made her realize that it wouldn't be safe for her to come at night. Tina asked if she would come by in the morning. "Okay," Anna said, "I will be there first thing in the morning." Anna promised she would be there at 6:00 a.m.

In the morning Anna got dressed and drove to East St. Louis to see Tina. Anna arrived. Tina was happy to see her, and she had a big smile on her face. "Hey, Sis," Anna said. "What's going on?" Tina said, "I just needed to see you, that's all!" They began to talk about the past, their adult children, the pain in her body, and they prayed. Tina didn't want Anna to leave, but she knew her little sister had to get back home for work. Tina walked Anna to the door. They hugged and said, "I'll see you later" to each other. As Anna was going out the door, Tina said, "Anna Jean, I love you, girl!" Anna turned around and said, "I love you too, Sis!"

Tina stayed in the door with it open; as she was slowly closing the door, Anna looked back and saw Tina looking at her through the cracked door. Anna said one more time, "I love you, Sis," thinking that maybe she should come back later. The door closed, and Anna drove back home, preparing to sign in to work. When Anna got home, just an hour or so later, the phone rang. Tina was gone! Tina had died of a heart attack shortly after Anna left. Their big sister was gone. God had allowed Tina to stay until she saw Anna one last time. That was the last prayer with her sister, the last talk with her sister, the last hug from her sister, the last look from her sister, and the last "I love you" from her sister. "I love you, Anna Jean," were the last words Tina spoke to her.

Anna questioned herself: "Maybe if I had stayed; what if I had taken her with me; or what if I had not gone to her house?" All of those questions ran through Anna's mind; still, she was thanking God that she had seen her big sister one last time. Anna hurried back to Tina's house, informing everyone that she was just there: "Tina is not dead, and this can't be true!

I was just with Tina!" Anna went to the hospital where Tina was. Tina was lying lifeless, more peaceful than she had ever been in her life. This news crushed Anna. Anna kissed Tina on the cheek, crying, asking, "What happened, Lord?" Anna said, "Lord, I don't understand! Why didn't you tell me, Lord, that you were going to take my sister? Father God, help us, Lord!" Anna had just lost Byron in November, and now Tina in April. "It hurts so bad," cried Anna. "I need your help! I can't take anymore, Father! Please, I can't take it! Help, Lord!" The day of Tina's funeral, after the burial, Anna had to immediately rush to the airport to get to Colorado to see Albany. Anna had to pull it together quickly.

DAUGHTER, ARISE!

Anna left the cemetery, and immediately after, they arrived at the airport to catch a flight to Denver, Colorado, to see her daughter, Albany. Albany, during childbirth, had started hemorrhaging. She was in critical condition. Anna was informed to get there ASAP. At that time, Anna wasn't thinking; she was still in shock, numb, and in disbelief that these things could be happening. All Anna could do was cry out, "Help, Lord, help!" Anna arrived in Colorado and was informed of a good report: a beautiful, new princess, Alayah, had been born. The Lord had answered Anna's prayers—her daughter was recovering well and was being prepared to be released from the hospital. Leaving death and arriving at a new life brought joy amid so much pain. All was well in Colorado! "Thank you, Jesus—You did it!" Now it was time to go back home to grieve the loss of Tina.

Anna arrived home to face the pain of the loss of her sister. Grief met her at the airport, as soon as she got off the plane. Anna was reminded of the day she had arrived home to receive the call that Tina was gone. She had to face reality. It was barely a month later that Anna lost her brother David, her father's other son by Ms. Martha, who was her fifth child. He had been in the hospital, sick with HIV (AIDS). All of this was overwhelming!

It didn't make sense—within seven months, Anna lost three siblings. "Oh my God, Father, what are you doing?" Grief and sorrow were hovering like a helicopter. Anna's siblings were dying one after the other. Byron, Tina, and David were no more. Anna began to seek God; she wanted to know: why? God was the only one who could answer that question. Anna had been informed, "You never question God." Yet it is written in Matthew 7:7 (KJV), "Ask, and it shall be given you; seek, and ye shall find; knock, and it shall be opened unto you." Anna did just that.

Anna began to fast, pray, and seek God's face on the deaths of her siblings. Skeeter was murdered; then Rochelle went to sleep (and never woke up—her heart stopped beating); Michael went up a hill and never came down (his heart stopped beating); Gary was found murdered; Byron became sick and was in the hospital—his organs shut down; Tina died of a massive heart attack due to high blood pressure and obesity; and David died of a sexual disease. Anna cried out to God for months for the breaking of generational curses, pleading the blood of Jesus, repenting for the sins of her father and ancestors. Everything that Anna thought could be the case, she did—then one night...

CHAPTER 5

REVEALED KNOWLEDGE

Call to Me, and I will answer you, and show you great and mighty things which you do not know.

Jeremiah 33:3

BREAK EVERY CHAIN

One night, while Anna was praying and crying out to God, she received an open vision. An open vision is like a movie, played out right before your eyes in prayer. In the vision, all of her siblings by her mother were lined up from oldest to youngest. There were Arthur Jr. (Skeeter, deceased), Carlton, Tina (deceased), Carolyn, Anna, Reginald, Bernadette, and Tyrone in a big, open, dark space. In this space there was a huge pair of scissors behind them, larger than they were, lowered from heaven. These scissors went to Skeeter first; they opened and closed behind him, cutting something. Anna couldn't see what it cut. The Lord had control of the scissors, though Anna never saw Him nor His hand. After it cut what was behind Skeeter, he smiled and waved goodbye to Anna, and he went up, wearing his uniform. He was so happy! Anna saw him one last time, then no more.

Then Carlton was cut; when it got to Tina, she looked at Anna and smiled, waving goodbye, and she went up. She was at peace; Anna saw her no more. Then the scissors cut Carolyn. When the scissors cut Anna, she felt the pressure of this invisible cord that the scissors had cut. This cord was thick and hard. Then Anna's younger siblings were cut by the scissors from heaven. The vision ended, Anna came to herself, and later she called her sister Carolyn to tell her what had happened. They cried! Anna believed that the cords were soul ties and generational curses from the sins of their father. Their father had hurt so many women that Tina believed that one of those women could have put a curse on him, his children, and children's children! Generational curses are real. Anna wondered why none of her father's children by the other women were in the vision.

Anna talked to her sister, Diana (Ms. Martha's daughter), informing her about the vision. Diana said, "She is in church and is praying for her family!" There were only her and Angela left of Ms. Martha's children by their Dad. For some reason, Anna knew there was a connection between their father's past and the loss of her siblings. We all need to pray for our unsaved loved ones. Never let your guard down. Sin has consequences! *Enough is enough!*

THE ENEMY COMES TO STEAL, KILL, AND DESTROY

During this time of trying to figure out what was going on with her family, Anna was experiencing depression, grief, confusion, and pain in her body. She didn't know what was going on. Two months after losing her brother David, someone broke into Anna's house. The night it happened, Anna was in class and had this feeling come over her that she needed to go home. It's that feeling you have when you think you left something cooking, but she hadn't cooked that day. When she pulled into the driveway, they ran from her home. They had gone through everything in her home. Every drawer was emptied; they were looking for cash and valuables. The police arrived and informed Anna that apparently whoever it was had been watching her coming and going. She had been led to go home early that night, which had prevented them from taking what they had left at the door! She no longer felt safe in her own home. Okay, here we go—Anna should've run!

A couple of months later, a man inquired of Anna after seven years of being single. Anna should've run! Anna had no desire to marry again. She just wanted God's will done in her life. Anna had no business saying yes; she was confused and grieving—a bad combination for a relationship or for making any major decisions. Anna sought the Lord's approval and was reminded that God would restore everything she had lost. But that didn't mean Raymond would be a part of the restoration process. Anna should've said, "*No, thank you!*" but she didn't! Anna and Raymond dated for six months, then married. After the ceremony, Raymond's mother looked at Anna and said, "I hope you are ready for this, because you got your hands full." Anna couldn't believe that his mother had come to her with a statement like that on the day of their wedding. Anna wouldn't have stopped the wedding, worrying about what others would have thought. That was only the beginning.

The next day Anna awakened to Raymond asking her, "Anna, do you remember the lady in the blue dress at the wedding?" Anna said "No, what lady?" He said, "The woman from my job. She didn't believe I would marry you." Anna said, "What?" He said, "I told her I would marry you." Then Anna realized that she had just made the biggest mistake of her life! "What have I done?" cried Anna. "What have I done?

Who does that?" Anna was set up by Satan! On top of everything Anna had gone through, now this! *Enough is enough*!

Anna continued to try to move forward. She couldn't tell anyone what she had fallen for. How had this happened to her? He continued to see this woman. Shortly after the wedding, Anna was diagnosed with lupus. Anna believed it was because she had married a man she should never have married. Raymond was a minister—his parents were the Pastor and First Lady of the church. He had been with most of the women in the church; that is what his mother had meant by that comment, "I hope you are ready for this, because you got your hands full." Anna needed time away, so she went to Colorado for a couple of weeks over the Thanksgiving holiday. When the cat is away, the dog will play—I mean, mice!

Anna arrived at the St. Louis airport. Raymond picked her up, and the atmosphere was so thick you could have cut it with a knife—an ax was more like it. No words were needed between either of them; the silence said more than words could ever say. When they arrived home, nothing had changed. Anna went into the bedroom to unpack, and she heard the Spirit of the Lord speak in a clear, still, small voice, "Do not sleep with him!" Raymond came into the bedroom saying, "I missed you!" Anna didn't respond. All she could hear was that still, small voice. That night Raymond went into the spare bedroom to sleep. During the night, Raymond got up to use the restroom; Anna heard the word "chlamydia." Anna said, "Lord, what? What is chlamydia?" The next day Anna looked online to figure out what chlamydia was. She didn't even know how to spell it. Anna called Raymond to ask if he had this. Raymond said, "No!"

Anna knew he was lying. The next day, she went to see a doctor for an STD test. She was negative for all tests, but he wasn't. Even though Anna had made a big mistake in marrying him, God had still protected her. The blood of Jesus had covered her! God had done it again! Anna asked Raymond to leave. It was over. Anna was looking at another failed marriage. The only thing Raymond said was, "It's not your fault; you did nothing wrong! Anna, you will find someone else!" Sounded familiar—were men trained to say that in the church? Anna didn't need him to tell her that. She needed people to stop playing games, because marriage is not the *Dating Game*! You're in the church, not the world! Saved—saved from what? Delivered—delivered from what? "Are you kidding me?" Anna said. The pain in Anna's body increased due to the stress of everything. She had lost three siblings in seven months, had had a home invasion, was diagnosed with lupus, and now this. Just stop! *Enough is enough!*

The divorce was final, and Anna wanted to forget everything that had happened in her life. Anna remembered the conference she had attended where there was a man of God who spoke and said during his message, "Don't you marry that man!" This just added guilt and shame to the list of pain Anna was carrying. That word was for her, and she had ignored it! She was the one who had said yes. She had disobeyed God! Anna was hurting; the shame and guilt were eating away at her. Anna was thinking that she was paying for leaving Minister Mitch, not realizing that years later, she would find out that he'd had a son with one of the women at their church while he was with her. Lord, no more shame and guilt! *Enough is enough!*

Satan wanted her to take her own life. Anna was listening to Satan, who is the accuser of the brethren, as he filled her mind with shame, guilt, and condemnation. Anna kept taking pain medication that day, one after the other, not monitoring or keeping count. She went to bed that night extremely medicated (drugged). Anna just assumed that she would sleep it off, not realizing how many pills she had taken. Anna was out—she had no idea for how long. Anna's heart had stopped beating! Anna had stopped breathing!

There was a voice from heaven that said to her soul, "Breathe, Anna!" God breathed life back into her again! Anna awoke, realizing what had happened. She was crying, afraid, shocked, and shaking. Anna heard the Spirit of the Lord's voice again, saying, "There is need of you!" Anna began to weep uncontrollably. She couldn't stop crying, realizing that her life had nearly been over. He had brought her back, after all the other people she had lost—but God had brought her back, allowing her to live. Anna cried, "Father, you still love me!" *I am the God who sees!*

Though Anna had disobeyed God, He still loved her! Psalm 139:8 (KJV) informs us, "If I ascend up into heaven, thou art there: if I make my bed in hell, behold, thou art there." She praised her God like she had lost her mind. Anna had stopped breathing; she was crying profusely. It's not over until God says it's over! Anna's deficit had pushed her closer to her destiny. Anna needed a new church home to be planted and rooted in.

WHERE COULD ANNA FIND

A SAFE PLACE?

Anna knew that it was time to find a church she could attend to find healing for her soul. All Anna wanted was a church to call home. Anna went to a church (No Name Church) that she thought would be the place. But Anna found no love from them; the women were jealous and grouped in cliques. The First Lady turned her nose up at Anna; Anna couldn't believe what she saw! Anna tried so hard to allow them to see her heart, not the way she looked. See, as you know, because Anna had not been reared in the church, she didn't understand their behavior. She was beginning to think that she wasn't missing anything! Anna wasn't created to be like you, nor were you created to be like her. We're created in God's image and likeness. Anna was a worshiper, and she expressed it affectionately. Once Anna received the Lord, she never lost her worship, because that is where she felt the safety of His arms.

It is written in Luke 12:48 (KJV), "But he that knew not, and did commit things worthy of stripes, shall be beaten with few stripes. For unto whomsoever much is given, of him shall be much required: and to whom men have committed much, of him they will ask the more." From him to whom much is given, much is required. God had given much to Anna, but not just natural things—He had forgiven Anna for so much that she was so thankful. The things that God had brought her out of were expressed. You really don't know how great God is until He brings you out of something that you can't get out of yourself. Anna was thankful and wanted to express that to others. In the Spirit, she washed His feet with her tears and dried them with her hair. It takes all that, and much more!

So, Anna decided she would do as the Word says and show herself to be friendly, which meant nothing to these ladies. What they didn't realize was that Anna wasn't looking for a man and surely didn't want theirs. She wanted peace and a place to belong. After being rejected by the men who said they loved her and the women who were jealous of her, the furthest thing from Anna's mind was to cause someone else pain!

The pain that Anna had experienced most of her life, she wouldn't have wanted for her worst enemies. Anna wanted to tell these women, "Not every single woman is looking for a man! We all need discernment! Remember, the Church is a hospital formed to restore His children to Him! All souls belong to God, and we must be careful about how we treat people. We might be entertaining angels unaware!" Anna had been through so much and didn't want to answer for that, too. Anna didn't want anyone's man or any attention; she just needed help! Anna at this time had been in the church for a while, but there are some who come who will not know church behavior. They will be the called-out ones—called out of darkness and needing emergency help (911)! Woe unto him that scatters God's sheep! They are the Remnant that will rise up after this pandemic! When you have done it to the least of these, you have done it unto me. Anna didn't say anything out of respect for their authority, and she knew that God would work it out.

Anna finally understood that everything that had happened was to get her where God wanted her to be. Anna found herself praying for these women, and as she did, she began to see change. Anna became a big part of their intercessory team, and God moved. Eventually, the First Lady of the church apologized, though Anna had already forgiven her. Then Anna prayed that God would allow her to move back to Colorado. After making so many mistakes doing things her way, she began to cry out to God, "Not my will, but Your will be done!" Anna's way was causing her a lot of pain and regrets. Colorado was where Anna's heart was, but how much more pain did she want to receive by her own hands? Anna decided she wasn't moving until God said so! *Enough is enough!*

THE KING OF KINGS IS NOT BURGER KING!

After numerous confirmations and finally hearing the voice of the Spirit of the Lord speak, "Yes, My will be done!" Anna started packing. Once Anna got the words "My will," it was a done deal. It was on now! Anna was able to rent out her house to a young lady with three kids. The young lady was a Christian and desperately needed to move from the area she was living in which was very, dangerous for her and her children. The family that God chose loved the new home and neighborhood. The only problem was that she couldn't afford it on her income. Anna sought the Lord on what to do. Anna knew that it was God's will for them to live in *His* house. Yes, *His* house—Anna only lived in it.

The young lady could only afford a few dollars over the mortgage payment, which was a little difficult for Anna for putting aside funds for unforeseen repairs and miscellaneous items. It was not enough, but Anna had to trust God's will. Anna was able to keep her job working from home, which transferred to Colorado. The only thing that didn't add up was the fact that Anna found it hard to make a living on Missouri's pay rate against Colorado's economy! It just didn't add up, *but God*! Anna believed God and continued to prepare for the move. She was on her way to Aurora, Colorado, where she had lived for thirteen years prior.

It was time to go back to her home away from home. Anna was loading the final things on the truck and had forgotten to remove her bedroom curtains. While Anna was standing on a stool, she was injured—her leg slipped and was over-extended. It was Anna's driving leg. Anna was in extreme pain; she could barely walk. She grabbed the curtains, loaded up the truck, and hit the highway. Anna felt that she couldn't do this. She just kept thinking about going home. She was determined to drive until she couldn't drive anymore! She was desperate to see her daughter and grandchildren. Anna at some point began to get sleepy; it was dark, and she heard the Spirit of the Lord say, "Anna, *wake up!*"

Anna was on the highway, weaving in a twenty-foot U-Haul truck, with a transporter carrying her vehicle. She pulled over, pulled herself together, and found her way to the closest hotel. It's 829 miles—twelve hours thirty-nine minutes—straight from Hazelwood, Missouri, to Colorado. God made sure that her sons, who were to help her drive, weren't able at the last minute to do it. No matter how badly they wanted to, their jobs wouldn't allow them the time off. That wasn't their job's doing. It was God! Psalm 118:8 (KJV), "It is better to trust in the Lord than to put confidence in man." It was a lesson Anna learned the hard way! Anna was alone on I-70, yet not alone!

Anna arrived in Colorado in one piece—only God! She was in excruciating pain, but she had made it by the grace of God. He kept her from all hurt, harm, and danger. She went to the hospital, was given a brace and medication, and then she went home and continued to unpack. You never know how strong you are until you are desperate enough to look past the pain. Anna had endured many horrific situations in her life, but this was a bit much. She remembered being on the highway with tears rolling down her face, asking Jesus to heal her leg so she could continue. She said, "If it is not Your will, help me endure this pain a little while longer." Anna, how badly do you want it?

ALL THINGS WORK TOGETHER

FOR GOOD

Anna realized that all things were working together for her good! Through "the good, the bad, and the ugly," the Lord was showing Anna who her Creator is. God was building her up for that which was to come. She didn't know what that was, but she was going to find out! In hopes of brighter days, Anna joined The Potter's House of Denver, which was a God move. The prayers of the righteous were availing much, and Anna became a big part of the intercessory prayer team. The life of praying for others was like a mantle to Anna.

Shortly after moving back to Colorado, Anna lost her sister Regina, her father's daughter by Ms. Nancy. She had been sick for a while. Like Anna, Regina had struggled with addictions to alcohol and drugs, as well. Anna had the opportunity to talk to Regina one last time when she was in the hospital. Anna was so happy to hear that the Lord had saved her sister. Regina was finally at peace, and Anna was able to tell her that she loved her so much. Here came death again, knocking at the door! Then a phone call from Anna's sister Carolyn seven months later informed her that Angela was dead. Her sister, Angela, had died. Angela was her father's daughter by Ms. Martha. Angela was Ms. Martha's sixth child to die!

Angela and Anna were so tight, and this hit her to her core. Regina's and Angela's deaths were seven months apart. So many loved ones were dying around Anna; the pain was so horrific. Anna remembered the laughs, the tears, the arguments, and the pain she had shared with her sisters. When these sisters were together, they set it off! Ms. Martha informed Anna that Angela had turned her life around by the grace of God. Angela had moved to another state, had joined a church, and was just baptized on Mother's Day. In less than a month, Angela died. She was gone!

Angela and Anna were tight, though it had been years since they had seen each other. The news was unbelievable! One sibling after the other—her pain felt unbearable, but she couldn't imagine Ms. Martha's pain. Anna was reminded of her mother—how she had lost seven babies, and she would have been the eighth by the hands of their father, but God had spared her. There had been so much death and loss around Anna. She couldn't help but think about how she must live for her siblings.

Financially, it appeared to be a struggle for Anna, living back in Colorado. Everything had changed. It wasn't that quiet little place anymore—the population had increased tremendously due to the legal approval of marijuana, which had caused the cost of living to skyrocket. It probably would have been easier for Anna to return to Missouri, but that wasn't God's will.

Anna was applying for jobs that paid more in her field, but no doors were opening. She couldn't understand why, but she continued to have faith in God. Anna was beginning to get behind on her rental property due to repairs on the property, paying the rent for her apartment, and other urgent needs that needed to be met. Anna was a faithful tithe and offering giver, which was due to her faith in God as a provider. She was giving back what belonged to Him; He only asks for ten percent, and you keep the ninety. You can't beat that!

Anna felt like her faith was on trial. She kept trying to get them to take some of the payment, and they wouldn't even take a partial payment. Anna only owed a little over $3,000. She had no place to get the money. "Father, help me," cried Anna. "I have done everything you told me to do, to the best of my ability!" Anna received a letter in the mail that read, "Your property shall go up for sale on April 9." Anna received this letter on April 6, three days before the selling of her home. The Lord had blessed Anna with this home. Anna screamed, "Father, my home, my house—Daddy, don't let them take my house!"

WHEN GOD CLOSES A DOOR,

IT'S CLOSED

Anna began to prepare to save her home from foreclosure. She was trying to get the money to fly to Missouri as soon as possible. All doors of opportunity to get the money were closed. The enemy was speaking in Anna's ear, "You are a loser!" Anna's son asked, "How could you lose our family home?" Shame began to overtake Anna. She wanted to borrow from her 401K, which was more than enough, but wasn't going to be accessible to her. She cried out again and again, "Father, help me! I need you—*help me, Daddy!*"

Suddenly, a still, small voice that she was very familiar with spoke, "Daughter, *let it go!*" She tried to deny what she had heard. "The devil is a liar! Father, that can't be you speaking, you had me to give away my other home and my limo. I have given away enough already," she cried, "and I have lost so much, Daddy—please, not this too! What about the family that's there, living in the home?" The Spirit of the Lord said to Anna, "I AM; I will provide!" He said, "*Let it go!*" Anna's home was gone. How did this happen? They sent letters stating, "Sold!" It was over! He had closed the door. The Lord's ways are not our ways, nor are His thoughts our thoughts.

The Lord had made sure that Anna wouldn't look back. He had closed the door so that she would never move back home. God knew her thoughts from afar off. He knew the intentions of her heart. Anna had wanted to keep her house so that she would always have a "just in case." A "plan B," just in case. Not her will, but God's will be done. Anna's destiny was in Colorado; she could visit Missouri, but never relocate. "It hurts, Lord," Anna cried. Anna's heart was broken! She began to question herself: "Was the enemy right—am I a loser? No, Satan is a liar!" She finally had to accept God's will. This was radical acceptance!

WHEN GOD SAYS GO, YOU GO

When God says no, you must move on. Anna moved on, trying to pick up the pieces of what was left, yet again. A couple of months later, Anna started a new job, surprisingly driving public transportation! It was always in her genes; she had just always avoided it. Anna's father drove public transportation for over twenty-five years, her brother Reginald had been driving over the road for thirty years, and her uncle had driven for over fifty-three years until his retirement. Anna loved driving, but this was the furthest thing from her mind. When God says go, you go!

Anna was being led to apply for a bus operator position with a local transit company. She didn't see this happening, but she applied. The words dropped into her spirit, "God did it!" The door was flung wide open. Her family was more surprised than she was. Not that she was happy about driving a bus, *but God*. Her family thought that she had lost her mind. See, Anna had worked in banking—from cashier to loan administrator, customer service, and the clerical field—for over thirty-five years. So yes, she was surprised! Finally, she realized that it was more than a job; it was a ministry.

Nothing Anna had gone through would be wasted. Getting past the crazy hours was difficult for Anna. She was exhausted! Working six days a week—up to ten hours a day, some days with only eight hours between the next shift—raised her prayer life to another level, indeed. Anna found herself crying out to God for help—not because of the money; it was great. Anna prayed before, during, and after to make it home from exhaustion. She was able to endure due to the fact that it was God's will for her. God's boot camp—you make it through this, Anna, you can make it through anything! Anna needed more grace.

Anna began to see things differently. She knew that if she complained, that only lengthened the process. So, she began to praise God like she never had before! "Trust and believe"— this brought the dogs out! Anna was beginning to declare war on the enemy camp. It was bad when she had to breathe in the smell of marijuana, cigarettes, alcohol, etc. Now, keep in mind that when all that's combined with an angry, hurt, emotionally challenged person, you had better have God to protect you! It became a ministry on the streets of Colorado. Anna was beginning to enjoy it when she saw it through the eyes of God.

God loved them! Anna no longer saw the homeless person, the drunk person, the angry person, nor the bitter person. She saw the hurting person, the lost person—and they were beginning to be happy to see her. She didn't judge; Anna just smiled and spoke, that's it! They didn't know it unless they asked, but she was praying for them. Anna would be driving up and down the streets of Colorado, praying. Driving these streets, she saw those living out of cardboard boxes, those passed out drunk, and those in so much pain that they could barely stand up. Prostitutes were boarding the bus, and drug dealers. God hates sin but loves the sinner! Women were being verbally and physically abused, and there were drug deals at the bus stop on Colfax; all you could do was pray! She had learned to quickly pull in and out, keeping it moving, to protect those who were on her bus.

Anna was heartbroken for the elderly, the sick, the lame, and the blind. They were using walkers, wheelchairs, canes, and dogs. The vision in her mind of her passenger who set himself on fire in the park on Colfax still brings pain to her heart. She would be driving and would have to wait until she got to the end of the route to let it out. She had to release the cry for the Father to heal, deliver, and set free. She was looking through the eyes of Jesus! That is why when He says go, you go. People are hurting! There is so much evil, and there is so much pain! ***Enough is enough! I am the God who sees!***

THE RIDE OF ANNA'S LIFE

It was just another busy day in the life of a bus operator. Anna was running about eight minutes late, and she had just started heading south on her last round trip of the day.

She stopped at a stoplight and this man ran up, beating on the door in the middle of the street. He was yelling, "Open the door! I been chasing you for the last couple of blocks!" Anna thought to herself, *Yeah, right!* She told him to go to the bus stop. He began to run back and forth in the middle of the intersection. Anna knew that something wasn't right! She was right—something was extremely wrong!

Anna pulled over to the stop and opened the door, letting off some of the senior passengers who warned her to be careful, and the man got on. Trust me: if Anna hadn't had to drop off her senior friends, she would have kept rolling right on past him. Anna informed the man, "Sir, please don't chase after a bus!" The man said, "Yes, ma'am!" At this point, the man's countenance changed the minute he took his first step onto the bus. See, Anna knew the urgency of prayer, praise, and pleading the blood of Jesus over her bus before and during her shift. What that man felt was the presence of God, and he thought he was clear of what he had done. Well, he wasn't!

Anna, back in motion, drove about two blocks down. All of a sudden, simultaneously: the man was yelling, "Open the door—let me off this bus"; passengers were screaming; the police were surrounding the bus while Anna was trying to stop so she didn't hit them; and the company dispatch operator was calling! Anna's left hand picked up phone and she heard a person yelling, "Stop the bus and open the door." Her right hand was on the steering wheel, her foot was on the brake trying to stop the bus, and her eyes were on the man using her rearview, as she silently cried out, "Jesssuuuussssss!" Her bus slowed down; she threw the phone down, stopped the bus, and opened the door. The man ran off the bus, dropping his backpack at the rear door. Numerous police, with guns drawn, shields up, rushed the bus and began to say, "Be still; don't move." They looked at Anna and said, "Don't move, and keep your hands on the steering wheel."

While the police were searching, they grabbed the backpack, and one of them said to Anna, "Did you know that he just robbed a bank?" Anna said, "What?" "Did you know that *he just robbed a bank?*" Anna said, "*No*, I just picked him up at the last stop!" They finally put their guns away, because the other police were chasing the bank robber. Anna was shaking and in shock, but didn't know it. The police began to tell her that they had caught him—he had a gun and knife on him, but the money was in the backpack that he had dropped. Who uses a bus as a getaway vehicle? Anna went on autopilot—she had to finish the route, dropping off passengers—and she collapsed when she got to the park-n-ride.

Anna was off work for five months, and in therapy for the trauma that she had experienced. She had to find the strength in Christ Jesus to move forward. Anna received just what she needed to go on, because Anna had become afraid of police, seeing people with backpacks, seeing people running, seeing buses, and hearing sirens—it would take her back to that moment. Anna began to speak the Word of God over her life that is written in 2 Timothy 1:7 (NKJV): "For God has not given us a spirit of fear, but of power and of love and of a sound mind." The power of God had risen up in Anna! She took back her life. Not only did she take back her life, but she also went back to that same route. Anna decided, "I have spent most of my life in fear; no devil in hell will have me bound by fear again!"

EYE IN THE SKY

Anna knew that God was with her every step of the way. Anna was working her Saturday 2:00 a.m. shift and was extremely exhausted. She began to call on the name of the Lord for strength in the wee hours of the morning. It always helped when the drivers who were feeling this way would pull the bus over, get out, and walk around the bus in the cool of the night to shake off the sleepiness. In this case, being a driver working a six-day mandatory workweek, it wasn't a surprise to be exhausted.

It was very early in the morning, with only two passengers who had boarded the bus thus far. Anna was driving westbound, facing the mountains of Colorado, and she began to get to the point where her eyes didn't want to remain open. She began quoting her favorite scriptures: "The joy of the Lord is my strength" and "Let the weak say they are strong!" Anna raised her eyes up toward the mountains; praying, as a tear fell from her eye, she quietly cried, "Help, Lord, help!" She stopped at a stoplight and there, in the sky, was one huge eye looking straight at her.

Anna couldn't take her eyes off of what she was seeing! She couldn't believe it—*Is it? It is!* She couldn't move, frozen in time. His voice spoke to her, saying, "I see!" Anna was in shock! As Anna was still sitting at the light, His eye began to close and started pulling back as if an eyelid was closing. The Lord wanted her to know, "I see!" It was one eye just for Anna! She spent the rest of her shift alert and strengthened, thinking, "The eyes of the Lord are upon the righteous, and His ears are open unto their cry" (Psalm 34:15 KJV). He heard her cry! He is the God who sees!

Anna was reminded of the glory of God. The manifested presence of God had shown up in the chapel of The Potter's House of Denver a year prior to the "Eye in the Sky." It was during the first service; Anna, Sister Lonnie, and Sister Esther were in the chapel praying for the service. All three of these women were standing at the altar. Worship was at an all-time high, and the glory was so thick—to the point where they could barely stand. Sister Esther's back was facing the west side of the church. Sister Lonnie's back was between the aisles, facing the south side of the church. Anna's back was facing the east side of the church. Suddenly, Anna looked over at Sister Lonnie, and she was walking backwards up the aisle, laughing as if someone was pushing her. Anna was trying to keep her focus on God, yet in awe of what was happening. Suddenly, Anna began to move backwards too—it was gentle, yet powerful. The glory of God was in that place, and He wanted us to know it. It was as if God took his hand and pushed us about fifteen feet. It was God; we had no control. Sister Esther was in awe, mouth wide open, wondering what had just happened to her sisters. When it was over we just looked at each other, praising God for what he had just done. *I am the God who sees!*

CHAPTER 6

SEVENTH MATTER
OF THE HEART

OH MY GOSH, DADDY!

Anna received a call from her sister Carolyn. Diana was gone; she had died! Diana was Ms. Martha's last child by their Dad. Diana had died of a broken heart because her mother, Ms. Martha, had died months prior, and all of her children by Anna's father were dead. Anna remembered the conversation she'd had with Diana, informing her to pray to break the generational curses that could've been over their families due to their father's sins. All Anna knew was that what God had done for her and her mother's children, He could do for them.

Anna had told Diana how the huge scissors from heaven came and cut the soul ties to their father off her siblings. Anna's father had beaten seven children out of her mother because he had wanted to be with Ms. Martha and her seven children by him. The seven children her father had beaten from Anna's mother were vindicated. Ms. Martha lost her seven children; they had died very suspicious deaths. Please, understand that neither Anna nor her mother had ever wanted anything like that, and that Anna loved that side of her family more than anyone would ever know. She loved them and loved being around them. There was no rhyme or reason for this trauma. **_Enough is enough_!**

Anna learned to understand that God is for the underdog, the afflicted, those that suffer by the hands of another. Some may call it "karma," and Anna didn't know why, but God does. Ms. Martha had to be alive to see six of her children die. It's believed that Ms. Martha knew what was going to happen next. Ms. Martha died, and shortly after Diana died. The last child between Anna's father and Ms. Martha was gone; all seven of their children had died premature, suspicious, and unexpected deaths. Woe unto him who afflicts pain on someone knowingly! **_Enough is enough_!**

Anna was trying to grasp that all of her siblings by Ms. Martha were gone: Rochelle, Gary, Diana, David, Angela, Michael, and Byron. These premature, suspicious deaths won't be ignored. The sins (curses) of Anna's father should've been broken years before. There was a spirit of murder, addiction, gambling, poverty, suicide, obesity, depression, illness, abuse, and premature death. Anna began to declare a decree: "Breaking every curse—every spirit that is not of God is to be broken off of my family lineage, every generation." Anna kept thinking about what could have been done differently to prevent the traumas her family had endured. What else could she have said?

It's hard to tell Anna's story, but this is a message for adulterers. You are opening the door to feeling the pain of that hurting spouse firsthand. Be careful of who you lie down with, because you will receive everything that could be attached to their life, be it curses or bondages. These women suffered horrific pain. Anna's mother's life was a life filled with pain. She never had the chance to live a good life. What God has joined together, let no man put asunder! **_Enough is enough_!**

WELL DONE, BIG BROTHER;

ENTER INTO GOD'S REST!

It was February 2018, and after fifteen years of fighting prostate cancer, Anna's brother Carlton knew it was time. Her brother Carlton was the father that their dad wasn't—or could never be. It's not that Carlton didn't have faults in the beginning, but he had found his way back home to his Father, God. Carlton sought God day and night. He loved talking about the Word of God, because he was on his third time reading and studying the whole Bible. He became the mother and the father for his children and siblings. He had endured many losses: their big brother Skeeter; Daddy, whom Anna never got a chance to know; Tina, their sister they grew up with; and many of his friends who had gone before him. Carlton loved his children and grandchildren so much; all those years, he went through the pain of chemo to be with them another day. Carlton's last words to Anna were, "Love God, and love people. I love you, Anna Jean!" Anna replied, "I love you too, Carl!" That was the last time Anna heard his voice; he died the next day. God will always send a sign, a miracle, or a wonder!

Only God! Anna was sitting in the Denver International Airport, waiting to fly home for her brother's funeral. She was posting on Facebook, talking about how her brother got his wings to fly home. At the same time, Anna was reading the passage Genesis 8:17 (NIV) in the Bible: "Bring out every kind of living creature that is with you—the **birds**, the animals, and all the creatures that move along the ground—so they can multiply on the earth and be fruitful and increase in number on it." Suddenly, the people sitting around her started talking to each other and looking at her feet. She looked at them and said, "What's wrong with my feet?" not looking down, because she was afraid. They said, "There is a baby bird at your feet." Then one lady said, "It's a baby sparrow." Anna jumped up—it flew to her seat, then it flew away. She saw a baby sparrow right after she sent that post about her brother getting his wings. Anna told the people around her what she was doing at the exact time it happened. They told her, "The bird flew down in front of you and was walking directly towards you, and stopped right at your feet." *Amazing God*! The people were in shock, and so was Anna! Sitting in the airport, she couldn't move. She sat there until she missed her flight. Anna didn't mind—it was a sign and a wonder from God!

GOD FIRST, FAMILY SECOND, BUSINESS THIRD

Anna tried to bring her focus back to God's business—if she took care of His business, He would take care of hers. God's business is His souls, and her business was her family. "Father, help me to continue to do Your will, and keep me focused," cried Anna. Anna knew that the Father's ways aren't her ways. When her family had lost two loved ones to suicide and many family members to unusual deaths, Anna continued to seek God for answers. The life we live affects more than our own! It affects the generations to come. Anna asked God on many occasions why someone wasn't there to teach her how to live. Anna had to learn about life as she went about her journey. Anna prayed that people would learn from the mistakes she had made.

Focusing even more on God and her family, Anna prayed that the Father God wouldn't let them leave this life without knowing Him, having a relationship with Him, and letting go of their past forever. With Anna's older son, Damion, there was a consistent prayer, cry, and fasting for his soul. When Damion's life was not pleasing to God, He made sure that he wouldn't come around her. Anna would leave messages on his phone, telling him how much she loved him. Eventually, Damion would call. He would hold things forever! If you didn't do or say what he wanted you to, he would withhold his attention from you. Anna experienced this a lot; it was his way of controlling people, but it didn't work. She had dealt with that spirit in her marriages, so she knew what it was. Anna thought that with love and kindness God had drawn her, and it would draw him.

Those moments with Damion were rare, because the lifestyle Damion was living at the time, he kept from Anna. Every time he was with Anna, she asked, "How are you doing, son?" Damion's answer to that question, even as a little boy, was always, "I'm good, Momma, I'm good!" Damion wouldn't tell her what he was doing until he was in trouble; even then, he wouldn't tell her the truth of the matter or the details. Anna may not have been the best mother, but she did the best with what she had. She had an instinct of knowing when something wasn't right with her children before they came to her for prayer. Damion was very protective of Anna, especially after Anna had made so many mistakes with men. He began to realize that his mother had been through hell, and God restored their relationship as mother and son! It was a Mother's Day surprise, which was one of the best of Anna's life!

Anna had just arrived home from work and the grocery store. She was still wearing her work uniform as a bus driver. She was in her bedroom, taking off her cap and shirt. Then, there was a knock on the door. It was one of those police knocks! Anna opened the door, and there stood her son Damion (it was his knock), tall as the doorway, saying, "What's up, Momma, who is that in here with you?" Anna said, "What? What are you talking about, Damion?" "Momma, I am parked on top of the garage, and I saw a man go into your home!" Anna started laughing. "No man entered this house! Boy, are you crazy?" Anna said, "That was me! I just got home from work and was wearing my uniform with my work cap!" Anna couldn't stop laughing. Damion said, "Momma, I called Albany and told her what I saw, and she is on her way here!"

Anna said, "Boy, are you crazy?" He said, "No, I thought you had a man—it's dark and I couldn't see!" Albany and the girls got there, and she rushed through the door, saying, "Momma, *you got a man in here?*" Anna had to fall out laughing, "No, Albany, it was me," said Anna, "I was wearing my uniform!" Anna knew then that her kids loved her and wanted to know what was going on in her life. "No, Jesus is all I need until he says otherwise," Anna said. "I've been there and done that. No, I'm good!" Damion said, "I came to give you your Mother's Day present. It's only $100. Happy Mother's Day, Momma!" "Thank you, son!" It wasn't about the money; it was the thought that counted. Damion wanted his mother to know that he hadn't forgotten about her this time. Anna had already received the best gift in the world. The love of a child for his mother was the best Mother's Day gift of Anna's life! Anna was about to experience another amazing weekend that made her feel like she was at the top of the world.

Damion would always tell Anna, "Momma, if you are going to work your business, *work your business, then!*" Now it was time to focus on her business, Anna thought. "My job is good, my relationship with my children is going amazingly well, my health is good, ministry in the prisons is going great, money is good—yes, time to invest in my business!" So, Anna booked a flight to Dallas, paid the registration for a cosmetic seminar, which was her first one, and made arrangements for a hotel—her director set her up as a roommate at the Omni Hotel—done!

Anna was at the most amazing place she could have ever imagined! She flew in on a Thursday in July. Everything was extravagant, and she had never been to anything like it—it was the greatest show on earth! The consultants received accolades and were crowned for their achievements. *My God*, Anna thought, *that could be me!* These women had worked so hard at making other women feel important. Anna became an ambassador for the Cosmetics Foundation, which gives millions of dollars for cancer research and domestic violence against women and children. Beauty surrounded Anna. It was like a scene from the pageants she had rushed home to watch on their black and white TV as a child. But Anna wasn't sitting in front of that television. She was there!

It was like a dream come true! Anna was in every training class she could be a part of, and she stored up every word of wisdom from some of the top achievers. Her eyes glistened. Anna was in *awe* of it all. It was one of the best weekends of her life, and she didn't want it to come to an end, but it did. Anna was beginning to feel like this was where she belonged! All her teenage life was spent dreaming of being a model with makeup, gowns, crowns, ribbons, and success. She felt no sorrow about not accomplishing what she had dreamed, because now she could help others feel as important from the inside out. The time had come for Anna to pack to go home the next day.

As Anna began packing the night before her departure, a feeling of unease and fear filled her heart. Anna looked at her roommates and told them, "I need to go pray!" She went into the bathroom and prayed, feeling it would ease her heart. She didn't receive an answer as to why she was feeling that way. In prayer, she covered her children and grandchildren with the blood of Jesus. After praying everything that came to her mind and heart, she got up off the floor from prayer and opened the bathroom door, knowing that she had to trust God. Whatever was going on or going to happen, God would see Anna through it. She trusted God with her whole heart! Anna realized that she had no control over anything or anyone.

The last day in Dallas, everyone was packed and eating the last meal before their flights. Anna had met some amazing, anointed, strong, successful women of God who believes in God first, family second, and business third. Some of the women gathered to pray for Anna's strength, family, direction/clarity, and her success in her cosmetic business. Anna felt their hearts, and the love of the Father. The conversations and advice became so deep, without anyone saying a lot of specific words. God was using them to comfort Anna before her storm!

THE WORST PAIN OF ANNA'S LIFE AWAITS HER

Anna arrived at the airport, thinking about how she needed to take what she had learned and apply it. She received a call from her daughter, who was trying to tell her something, but she didn't understand what Albany said. Then they were disconnected. Anna's reception on her phone was bad at that airport. Little did Anna know that God was in control of blocking the information that she shouldn't receive in Dallas. Anna finally arrived at Denver International Airport and received a message from the children's uncle, Joe, that he was picking her up from the airport instead of Albany. Anna got her luggage and found Joe. Joe revealed that Albany was at the hospital with Damion! Anna kept asking Joe what was wrong with Damion. Joe was providing little to no information, but as he drove, her heart was still feeling unease. Anna remembered how she had felt the night before. She was scared, but she kept telling herself he'd be all right, no matter what was wrong.

Anna arrived at the hospital and was approached by Albany, who began to take Anna to the chapel. Albany wouldn't tell Anna what was wrong until she got her alone in the chapel. Albany said, "Momma, Damion is dead!" "What did you say?" "Momma, Damion is dead!" Anna screamed—*a cry that had no words!* Screaming, screaming, crying, and screaming was all that Anna did! Anna told her, "*No,* take me to my son!" Anna had this gut-wrenching pain, like someone had snatched out her heart. Albany said, "They won't let us see him, Momma!" Albany said, "Momma, I'm sorry, Damion was shot! They won't let us see him! It's an investigation!" Anna lost it! "The police need to check his fingerprints to make sure it's him!" "JESSSUUUSSSSSS!" Anna screamed.

Anna told everyone, "This can't be my son! Not one of you have seen him, so how do you know it's him?" Anna cried, "LET ME SEE MY BABY! LET ME SEE MY SON!" The nurse said, "The medical examiner will let the police know, and they will contact you. I'm sorry, you will have to wait!" Anna refused to believe that it was her son. Anna began to think about the day before she had left Dallas, the feeling of something not right—the sick feeling of fear that had consumed her. She remembered how she had prayed, pleaded, and applied the blood of Jesus over her children, grandchildren, on everything that came to mind. Anna had been in one of the happiest times in her life and had dropped to the lowest, most painful time in her life, all in the same day!

Anna was calling Damion's phone and praying that he would pick it up. Days went by, and then they got the news that *it was Damion!* All heaven broke loose in Anna. It was as if Anna's life had ended. Her pain felt like it was more than she could bear. Damion's life was over! No, we as Christians don't grieve as the world grieves, but the pain is just the same when you lose a child. *Horrific!* For the world, there is no hope of ever seeing your loved one again, but as Christians, we will in heaven! The life that Damion had lived was not one that God approved of, but little did Anna know that God had answered her prayers. Anna's prayer was for God to save her children: "Don't let them die without a relationship with You!" Once

Damion had told Anna, "Just because I don't go to your church doesn't mean I don't have a relationship with God!"

The next day Anna and Albany went to Damion's house; she needed to be close to him in some way. When she got to Damion's, there on the table was his Bible. The Bible had a church program from My Father's House with a recent date on it. In his Bible on the last page, in his handwriting, there was one scripture: 2 Corinthians 5:17 (NKJV), "Therefore, if anyone is in Christ, he is a new creation; old things have passed away; behold, all things have become new." Jesus had saved her son! As people began to share about Damion, everyone shared how he had begun to apologize for the bad things he had done to people. The Father had been working behind the scenes! God took him when his heart was the purest it would ever be. It was the prayers of his mother that had caused him to call on God months before he died.

Anna and Albany walked outside to the location where he was shot down. Anna began to call her son's name out loud at the exact place where he'd lain. Anna heard his voice say, "I'm good, Momma, I'm good!" Anna knew her son's voice and his favorite statement to his mother. Anna cried and began to thank God for letting her hear his voice say he was good! Anna began to find out the details, though no one saw what happened except the two involved. Damion had died because he loved her. Damion had come home early to find his girlfriend of six years with her lover, a block from his home. An argument had broken out, and the man had shot him. Damion had no weapon on him—not in his car, nor in his home. ***Enough is enough***! Stop the violence!

Damion died on a Monday, four days before his fortieth birthday. Anna was finally able to see her son that Saturday. He looked good—handsome as always, and there was such a peace over him that was unexplainable. Damion was dressed in the clothes he loved wearing and had on his favorite cap. That was the hardest day of their lives! Anna had been the first to kiss Damion when he came into this world, and she was the last to kiss him in death. She didn't see the man—she saw her baby, her boy, her child that had come from her womb. She remembered the kicks, and his eyes as a baby when he would look up at her with the love (agape) of God. A mother's love is like no other. Anna bent down, kissed his face, and said, "Damion, I love you, always and forever." Her daughter Albany on one side, and Damion's oldest son, Damion Jr., on the other side, said goodbye while closing Damion's casket. It was the last time she would ever touch her son's face. *Enough is enough*!

DAMION, YOU LAY, AND YOU TAKE MY BREATH AWAY!

WHY NOT YOUR SON?

After the funeral, Anna did an altar call, and numerous souls gave their lives to Christ. There were a couple of hundred people at his funeral from all walks of life. He had made a huge impact on so many lives. Damion was so loved. His life and death drew those who may never have gone to a church. The people heard the Word of God preached, and many answered the call. God will give the increase. 1 Corinthians 3:6 (KJV), "I have planted, Apollos watered; but God gave the increase." The death of Jesus saved many. The death of Damion made many realize that they needed Jesus!

All lives matter to God, but all lives don't matter to people! Dr. Martin Luther King stated, "None of us are free until we all are free!" The Black Lives Matter movement is because of the inhumane treatment and injustices they have endured for over four hundred years—since 1619—because of the color of their skin. Does that remind you of another group of people, like the Israelites' four hundred years of slavery by the Egyptians? My black and brown brothers and sisters, when will your black and brown brother and sister matter to you? Why have you become your oppressors? Since you say "all lives matter," stop the stealing, killing, neglecting, abusing, raping, adultery, degrading, drug dealing, manipulating, and sex trafficking! The prisons are filled with mothers and fathers whose children are left with devastation! What are you doing? The children are lost, the families are hurting, and they need you! The mother's tears have become her meat night and day. Anna spends weekends ministering to those who are in prison. She knows, she sees, she feels their pain. Wake up! Hurting people hurt people! Someone has hurt them, and now there is a domino effect. ***Enough is enough! I am the God who sees!***

Be not deceived; God is not mocked—whatsoever we sow, that shall we also reap (Galatians 6:7). Anna's father reaped what he sowed. He took the lives of seven embryos/infants, and he lost seven children, one after the other. Though her father didn't see it, Anna was number eight, but she was brought back to life to tell the story! They were all matters of the heart. The hearts were ripped out of both mothers' chests as they cried for their babies who died. Time is running out! Repent for the remission of your sins and turn from your evil ways! ***Enough is enough! I am the God who sees!***

Husbands and wives, lie down in your own beds; the grass isn't greener, it's just artificial! Where are the mothers? Your daughters need you. Men—rise-up and take your place; your sons and daughters need you. If you don't tell them who she is or who he is, someone else will, and it may not be good. Stop producing all of these children if you can't parent them. Don't play if you can't stay. Your sons were never meant to fill your shoes! ***Enough is enough!*** Stop the violence!

FROM THE WOMB TO THE TOMB

Anna went from the womb to the tomb! Anna learned obedience by the things she suffered; she learned respect for life, compassion for those in pain, and forgiveness, because hurting people hurt people. Anna had also hurt people. Her tears had become her meat night and day. It was very hard for Anna to accept the fact that Damion was gone and never coming back. One of the hardest things she had to do was to forgive the man that took her son's life. Anna had to die to her life again and again. She died daily!

Anna asked God, "Why?" He said to Anna, "It's for My glory; I will get the glory out of this." Jesus died for Damion. He died for her son's murderer too. Anna forgave him. She had to, because God said so! Now she prays for his soul, for his children, and that God gets the glory out of his life. She forgave the woman who had been in her home with her son weeks prior, smiling in her face while she was seeing a married man behind her son's back, which cost him his life. May God have mercy on their souls! Christ died for us all! We are born to die daily. 2 Chronicles 7:14 (KJV), "**If my people**, which are **called** by **my** name, shall humble themselves, and pray, and seek **my** face, and turn from their wicked ways; then **will** I hear from heaven, and will forgive their sin, and will heal their land." *Enough is enough! I am the God who sees!*

Anna had to continue to do the work of the Lord. Staying focused on what God had given her to do wasn't easy. She had to remember that this was all about souls. His souls must be saved! Anna could've easily crawled into bed, covering her head, but she had to get up. Anna wouldn't have realized that in her weakness, God is made strong! Anna continued to lose loved ones and understood fully that it was not her will, but God's will that would be done. It was through the blood of Jesus, in the love she had for God, and for her loved ones that she had to press her way through the pain.

Pressing past the pain and tears was something that Anna knew she had to do for her family. Just a few months later, Anna received word that the patriarch of their family had passed away. Her uncle had gone home to be with the Lord; and months after that his son, her cousin, passed away. After the loss of her son Damion, her grandson Damion Jr.'s sister Angel was murdered. Angel was twenty years old when she was murdered in Denver by someone who wouldn't accept no for an answer. *Enough is enough!*

Violence took the mother of a beautiful daughter; a beautiful daughter away from her mother; a loving sister away from her sisters and brothers; a caring granddaughter from her grandparents; and a fun, compassionate, devoted friend from all of her friends and family members. Anna's grandson, Damion Jr., one of Damion's children, lost his father and his sister within nine months of each other. Devastation tried to rip that family apart, but they allowed love to have her perfect work and to bring them all together. *Enough is enough!*

God gave Anna supernatural grace, peace, and strength to preach at the women's prison. To preach to women who may have done or been accused of doing the same type of crime her son Damion and step-granddaughter Angel had endured—murder. That is why unforgiveness wasn't an option for Anna. Anna had to die to her feelings and do the will of her Father, God. At Angel's funeral, over two hundred souls gathered in the church to say goodbye, and over a hundred gave their lives or rededicated their lives back to Christ. To God be the glory! Angel was so loved that there was not even standing room left; people were lined up outside the door to pay their respects. There is not a day that goes by that they don't mourn their loss. Anna and her family's lives will never be the same. Her grandson's life is a life spent without his father and his sister due to violence. All souls belong to God, and you own no one! No one is your possession. ***Enough is enough!*** *I am the God who sees!*

IT'S RESTORATION TIME

It is written in the King James Version of the Bible, in Joel 2:21-26:

> **Fear not, O land; be glad and rejoice: for the LORD will do great things. Be not afraid, ye beasts of the field: for the pastures of the wilderness do spring, for the tree beareth her fruit, the fig tree and the vine do yield their strength. Be glad then, ye children of Zion, and rejoice in the LORD your God: for he hath given you the former rain moderately, and he will cause to come down for you the rain, the former rain, and the latter rain in the first month. And the floors shall be full of wheat, and the vats shall overflow with wine and oil. And I will restore to you the years that the locust hath eaten, the cankerworm, and the caterpillar, and the palmerworm, my great army which I sent among you. And ye shall eat in plenty, and be satisfied, and praise the name of the LORD your God, that hath dealt wondrously with you: and my people shall never be ashamed.**

God is restoring everything that Anna and her family have lost. Anna is free! She is finally free to be who God has called her to be. *But God*! It is written in John 8:36 (KJV), "If the Son therefore shall make you free, ye shall be free indeed." Amen! She is *free*! She is free from abandonment, abuse, addiction, bondage, condemnation, depression, failure, fear, generational curses, guilt, lack, poverty, neglect, oppression, rejection, shame, sickness, ungodly soul ties, victim mentality, and yokes. He stays the hand of the enemy when He has a divine purpose for your life, with no more barrenness and no more spiritual abortions. You will live out your full and complete life! God is the Alpha and the Omega; He knows the end from the beginning. *Enough is enough*! *I am the God who sees*!

CONCLUSION: WHEN DESTINY COLLIDES WITH PURPOSE

As I began to finish this book, I, as the author, began to ask the Lord why I was supposed to do this now. "Father, You are healing, rebuilding, and transforming Your people, the family, and the church. Men are becoming better husbands, fathers, and men. Women are becoming better wives, mothers, and women. The church is beginning to go back to preaching on sin, the positions in the family, order in the family, and making God the head of the family. The church is raising up men and women that are taking back their families. Fathers are becoming more "girl dads" after the loss of the beloved Kobe and Gigi Bryant, and the others who lost their lives for the love they had for their children and others' children. They're focusing on generations and legacy. Father, why wasn't I allowed to write this book years ago?" Then the answer came!

I pulled up at a fast food drive-thru to get a bite to eat after work. I don't eat out like that. This was a God move! Yes, God is moving, no matter what it looks like right now. That morning it dropped into my spirit that I would leave my phone at home, so to make sure I didn't I sat it right next to my purse. Well, I did leave it! I didn't go back to get it, because I wasn't supposed to have it that day. I was sitting there thinking how leaving my phone at home earlier that morning wasn't so bad after all. I had survived it! *Hello!*

In the drive-thru there was an SUV in front of my car that was rocking excessively—little did I know that the driver of the vehicle was reaching into the back seat and beating a woman. She was telling him not to do that! I could see through the back window every time he would swing and hit her, even though the windows were tinted. Though there was a man in the front seat, he did nothing to stop him from beating her. She got ready to get out of the car and the other man said, "I got her."

I reached into my purse to grab my phone and remembered it wasn't there. I heard God's voice saying, "Be still and know that I am God!" They pulled up to the drive-thru window and I thought to myself, *That person at the window will see.* The abuser told her to shut up; as soon as the drive-thru window opened you could hear nothing from the SUV. The woman in the back seat said nothing. Then it was quiet! He paid for the food, the window closed, he hit her again. The window opened, they got their food, argued, and left. Help, Lord, help! *It's hidden in plain sight!* That's why He wants this book written. Just because we don't see it doesn't mean it isn't happening. ***Enough is enough! I am the God who sees!***

Let's discuss another horrific event: the husband in Missouri who killed his wife and two sons because he wanted to be with another woman. This was a family in the church! He had previously held a position to protect the people in that church, yet he murdered his whole family due to the lust of the flesh, lust of the eye, and the pride of life. Recently, in February of 2020 in Canada, a man killed his wife and three children. This was a Christian family! We must be the example to the world that our God reigns. Pray in faith and pray the Word of God. Father, in the name of Jesus, save, heal, and change the heart of man—so we can be safe in our own homes, so we don't have to sleep with the enemy, so citizens can be safe while they exercise by running in their own neighborhoods, so people don't have to worry about being able to breathe when they come out of a store. *Enough is enough!* *I am the God who sees!*

We must push: "Pray Until Something Happens"! "If my people, who are called by my name, will humble themselves and pray and seek my face and turn from their wicked ways, then I will hear from heaven, and I will forgive their sin and will heal their land" (2 Chronicles 7:14 KJV). This is not just a 'hood thing; it's not just the poor or drug addicted; it's not just black or white; it's in the corporate world, white collar, blue collar—it's in Hollywood: "#MeToo"! What goes on in the dark comes to the light. God doesn't care who or what you may think you are; *He sees!*

Prayer changes things, and the blood of Jesus still works! The fathers and mothers are so consumed with their lives that they don't know their daughters and sons are hurting, with suicide and school shootings running rampant. We have been pre-occupied with the things of the world, losing our focus to watch and pray. Countless children and young adults have come up missing all over the world for sex trafficking. What about the countless drive-by shootings of children just wanting to play outside in their own yards? Children are lost because there is no one to show them the way. Parents, don't just talk it, walk it! Prayer still works—cover them under the blood of Jesus!

Let's pray against the spirits: murder/homicide, violence, crime, assassination, hatred, racism, premature death, injustice, retaliation, suicide, abuse, anger/rage, and prejudice. We must be doers of the Word, because they are watching us! How are they going to trust someone whom we don't trust? God is the God of generations! Thus saith the Lord, "And he shall turn the heart of the fathers to the children, and the heart of the children to their fathers, lest I come and smite the earth with a curse" (Malachi 4:6 KJV). *Enough is enough! God is the God who sees!*

Jesus is risen, and we must rise up and take our place as the body of Christ who has all authority which is given to us by God. We must go and snatch them out of darkness, bringing them into this marvelous light. We must get tired of being tired of experiencing and hearing of tragedies. It's time for change! Be tired of living beneath what God has created for us, our families, and His people! Your past does not dictate your future. There is a more excellent way. It's time for order to come back to the church, back to the family, and back to the house. This book is written for those who will pray against the violence, hatred, and deception that has fallen on this land— hidden in the dark!

This commandment He gives unto us in Matthew 22:37-40 (KJV) informs us, "Jesus said unto him, Thou shalt **love** the **Lord thy God with all thy heart**, and **with all thy soul**, and **with all thy mind**. This is the first and great commandment. And the second is like unto it, **Thou shalt love thy neighbor** as **thyself**." Let the love of God penetrate your very soul, so you can learn to love and respect yourself. Love your family and others. What's love got to do with it? It's got everything to do with it! Oneness with God the Father, the Son, and the Spirit in Jesus' name is the more excellent way. Father God, bring back Your glory; release Your glory upon Your people! Bring back Your glory, God—Your manifested presence! For God to do this, there must be a true repentance before restoration. There has been a wakeup call! Answer the call! God is faithful and just to forgive you! Surrender to God; resist the devil, and he will flee from you. It's not where you start; it's where you finish. If you ask God to forgive you for your sins, they are forgiven, and your sins are thrown into the sea of forgetfulness too. Just pray this prayer, called "The Sinner's Prayer":

Heavenly Father, I come to you in prayer, asking for the forgiveness of my sins. I confess with my mouth and believe with my heart that Jesus is Your Son, and that He died on the cross at Calvary that I may be forgiven and have eternal life in the kingdom of heaven. Father, I believe that Jesus rose from the dead, and I ask You right now to come into my life and be my personal Lord and Savior. I repent of my sins and will worship You all the days of my life! I confess with my mouth that I am born again and cleansed by the blood of Jesus! In Jesus' name, Amen.

Enough Is Enough!
I AM THE GOD WHO SEES!